STOP
MEMORY
LOSS

STOP MEMORY LOSS

HOW TO FIGHT FORGETFULNESS OVER FORTY

MATTESON BOOKS
PACIFIC PALISADES, CALIFORNIA

Copyright 1997 William Cone, Ph.D.

Cover Design by William Cone
Text design by Paul Matteson

First Edition, September 1997

Publisher's Cataloging-in-Publication Data

Cone, William
  Stop Memory Loss : how to fight forgetfulness over forty / [by William Cone]. -- 1 st ed.
  p. cm.
  Includes bibliographical references and index.
  Preassigned LCCN: 97-92937
  ISBN: 0-9655563-9-5

  1. Memory disorders--Age Factors. 2. Memory--effects of drugs on. 3. Memory in old age. I. Title

  RC394.M46C66 1997   618.97'684
                               QB197-40599

Printed in the United States of America
10 9 8 7 6 5 4 3 2 1

Matteson Books
PO Box 332
Pacific Palisades, CA 90272

To Carolyn, and to Don Re, who both made this book possible, and to all of the people who have helped me, and yet tragically cannot remember doing so.

Humanity I love you
because you are perpetually
putting the secret of life
in your pants
and forgetting it's there
and sitting down on it

e. e. cummings

*The first thing an executive must have
is a fine memory.*

*Of course, it does not follow
that the man with a fine memory
is necessarily a fine executive.*

*But if he has the memory,
he has the first qualification.
And if he has not the memory,
nothing else matters.*

Thomas Alva Edison

ACKNOWLEDGMENTS

This book is the result of over twenty years of conducting memory improvement seminars. Over these years, countless hundreds of people have shared bits and pieces of information, each of which was added to my arsenal of ideas. I wish to acknowledge anyone whose ideas have found their way into these pages.

I would also like to thank Dr. Richard Leek and Dr. Mike Arnold for graciously checking the accuracy of the nutritional information. An additional thanks to Robin Quinn for being a tolerant editor, and to Paula for the index.

A NOTE TO THE READER

I am not a Medical Doctor nor a Nutritionist. The ideas and information presented in this book are not meant as a substitute for professional medical care or guidance. None of the supplements, herbs, vitamins, or medications herein should be taken or discontinued without first consulting a competent professional.

TABLE OF CONTENTS

CHAPTER ONE

MEMORY LOSS

It is not until we begin to lose our memory that we think very much about it. Even though we may complain at times about how bad our memory is, for the most part, we take it for granted. Aside from a forgotten name or a missed appointment, we pay scant attention to this truly magical quality of the mind.

But even though we take little notice, memory actually begins to decline as early as our mid-30s. The decline is so gradual that it doesn't usually become noticeable until our 40s, and doesn't really begin to plague us until our 50s.

In 1986 the National Institute of mental health defined this gradual decline in memory as *Age Associated Memory Impairment* (AAMI). AAMI is not a disease. It's not caused by strokes, by dementia, or by any other medical condition. It *is*, however, a gradual decline in several components of memory.

It is Age Associated Memory Impairment that causes us to stop in mid-sentence to grope for a word, one well known but temporarily unavailable. We call our children by the wrong name, and find ourselves adding "thingamajig," "whatsit," and "you know what I mean" to our daily vocabulary.

We may pause for a moment in conversation, only to lose our train of thought completely. As a rush of anxiety passes

1

through us, we ask our companions, "What was I just telling you?"

We invite our children for dinner, and as we begin to share an exciting piece of information, someone rolls their eyes and says, "You already told me that twice, Mom."

There is a gradual decrease in the speed of the memory process itself—retrieval takes longer. We see the face of a well known celebrity on the television, but cannot remember her name. But three days later, the now unwanted name comes to mind instantaneously.

Because of these problems, we begin to rely on others to store our memories. We tell them, "Don't let me forget to pick up the laundry," and ask, "What was the name of the movie I saw last night?"

By 50 we begin to notice that younger people learn new skills more quickly than we do. New areas of knowledge, new technology, new ideas, and frequent change become overwhelming and unwelcome, and we fall back on habit and routine to compensate for our newfound sense of inadequacy. We cope with this difficulty by calling new methods "newfangled," and we tell our children, "That's the way I've always done it, and I'm not going to change now."

As we age, we sleep less, and consequently dream less, which results in a more fuzzy recollection of days gone by. The plot of the movie we saw only two days ago eludes us, while one we saw ten years ago pops into our heads without effort. We can tell someone what we did fifteen years ago, but not fifteen minutes ago. For this reason the years begin to rush by, and we increasingly ask ourselves, "Where did the time go?"

We find ourselves standing motionless in the kitchen, at a complete loss for why we are there. Frustrated, we return to the den, only to suddenly recall the lost purpose of our fruitless and embarrassing journey.

We find ourselves more easily distracted—it becomes harder to concentrate when too much is happening at once. We compensate for this by keeping stimuli at a minimum. Crowds, parties, and crowded freeways become a strain on the system. "Turn that music down!" and "Keep those kids quiet!" become the mantras of maturity.

It becomes more difficult to do several things at once, or to execute a smooth transition from one task to another. This difficulty in stopping one task and beginning another is called *perseveration*.

And we keep losing things! We walk into the living room, intending to put our keys down on the end table, when suddenly we think of that last piece of cake in the refrigerator. With keys still in hand, we open the refrigerator door.

As we reach to in pick up the cake, we finish our first task—putting the keys down—by placing them on the top shelf next to the milk. Later, when we need the keys, we look on the end table and notice they are missing. "Who took my keys?" we cry in frustration.

And so we lose our keys, our concentration, and eventually our peace of mind. These memory problems huddle in the back of our awareness; subtle but insidious—temporary, but troubling. As we feel our memory slip, we begin to worry, "Is it finally happening? Am I getting senile?"

In the vast majority of cases, the answer is a resounding no. The problems just described are not warning signs of serious memory problems. In addition, many of these problems are reparable. In many cases these problems are not caused by disease or cell death, but are a result of nutritional deficiencies, medication problems, depression, thyroid imbalance, alcohol and drug abuse, and lack of care. As we shall see, diseases such as Alzheimer's and other dementias are rare.

WHAT CHANGES WITH AGE	WHAT DOESN'T CHANGE
Attention span gets shorter	Short term memory
Reaction time slows down	Memory for symbols
Attending to multiple tasks becomes difficult	Retrieval techniques
There is a need for reduced stimulation	The ability to learn
	Intelligence
Thinking processes are slower	Musical and artistic memory

It is a popular belief that the brain loses millions of cells each year. However, the scientific evidence does not support this common notion. But some cells *are* lost, and unfortunately for us, the brain cells that are most vulnerable and easily injured are located in the *amygdala* and the *hippocampus*; two parts of the brain that are essential for memory storage and retrieval.

Studies show that brain cells begin to die at an early age. After forty, the hippocampus loses about 5% of its cells every ten years. As a result of this cell loss, the average, healthy eighty-year-old has about two-thirds of the hippocampal cells that they had when they were born.

The hippocampus is necessary for the storage of facts, but not procedures. For this reason, people with damage to the hippocampus lose the ability to learn new information, yet they can still learn and remember new skills.

Some memory problems may be caused by the fact that the brain shrinks with age, and each aging cell contains less water, making metabolic functions more difficult. For this reason, proper nutrition and fluid intake are very important.

Other memory problems are thought to be caused by a

decrease in the amount of certain brain-cell chemicals called *neurotransmitters*. For example, the death or malfunction of hippocampal cells results in the decrease of an important neurotransmitter called *acetylcholine,* which is essential for learning and storing new material. Many treatments for memory problems center around increasing the level of this substance.

Although these changes in the brain do cause memory to slow down, in truth, normal aging does not destroy the ability to learn or to remember. An eighty year old is just as capable of learning a new skill as an eight year old, it just takes longer. Just knowing this can reduce anxiety and concern about your memory.

Even though brain changes may impair memory, we know that most memory problems are caused by the lack of effort to maintain and improve one's memory. The people with the best memories are those that use memory skills and techniques throughout their lives, and those who take proper care of the machinery of the mind.

This book is about minimizing memory loss, and reversing, eliminating, or slowing the most common causes of memory failure. Please read every page carefully, for you may discover something that will allow you to preserve the treasured traces of your past.

CHAPTER TWO

THE MANY TYPES OF MEMORY

One problem researchers have with studying memory is that there are actually several types of memory, and each type works differently. Of particular interest are the many types known as *sensory memory*—the memories we take in through our senses. Our eyes, ears, and other receptors take in data from the outside world and store it in ways we are just beginning to understand.

SMELL MEMORY

At the base of the brain are two tiny tubular bits of tissue called the *olfactory tubercles*. These tiny bundles of cells are the most primitive parts of our brains, and are responsible for our sense of smell.

Memory for smells is called *olfactory memory*. Most of us possess a fantastic ability to remember smells. We can recognize the smell of bacon frying, and tell the difference between that odor and the smell of ham frying, although the odors are very similar.

As children, we are very sensitive to smells, and many of our earliest childhood memories are, in fact, smell memories.

Each one of us has our own unique set of olfactory memories, and once recorded, a fragrance is seldom forgotten.

Even though many decades have passed, you might still remember the smell of fresh baked bread from your Grandmother's kitchen (as I do), or exactly how your favorite blanket or teddy bear used to smell. You might also recollect the way Aunt Beula's house smelled on Sunday afternoon, or how you hated the smell of steamed Brussels sprouts.

Although these memories are stored permanently, it may take a reminder to bring them into consciousness. In one of my memory seminars, a young woman told me a story about one of her olfactory memories. One day while she was doing her laundry, the drier broke. She took a load of wet T-shirts out of the washer, and hung them in the backyard to dry. Later that day, she went out to gather them. The moment she smelled the sundried clothing, she remembered sitting in her father's lap as a little girl, and smelling his fresh, sun-dried shirt. This was an event she had not thought about in thirty years.

Environment has a measurable effect on early smell memories. When researchers asked people to recall early olfactory memories, they found that people born between 1900 and 1929 remembered the childhood smells of nature. Those memories included the smell of horses, hay, sea air, pine, and meadows. Those born between the years 1930 and 1979, however, reported memories of the smells of Vick's VapoRub, plastic, Magic Markers, Play-Doh, and Sweet Tarts. Technology had replaced nature.

Researcher Fred Bryant asked his students to recall pleasant smell memories form childhood. He then exposed them to the odors, and found significant increases in the recall of pleasant memories. More importantly, he found that the enjoyable memories improved the mood of the person remembering them.

Exercise: Wake up and smell the roses

Pleasant odors, such as cinnamon and oranges, elicit positive childhood memories and other pleasant recollections in most people. You can use this process to soothe yourself the next time you're feeling down. You just need to make a few preparations first.

♦ Make a list of all the pleasant smell memories you can recall

♦ Reproduce the fragrances

♦ Make yourself a "fragrance kit" by putting these fragrances in small bottles

♦ When you need a lift, expose yourself to the scents

Apparently "wake up and smell the roses" is a saying with hidden benefits.

In a third study researchers discovered that the recollections of the odors of childhood were related to how one felt about their early years. Those with unhappy childhoods were most likely to recall unpleasant odors.

The ability to smell is often damaged in people with Alzheimer's disease. In fact, long before Alzheimer's sufferers begin to show memory impairment, they lose their ability to recognize odors.

But Researcher Michael Serby felt that it was not the sense of smell itself that was defective in Alzheimer's patients. He decided to look at the ability to *detect* the presence of an odor compared to the ability to *identify* the odor. The results of his study showed that even when people were able to detect an odor, recognizing and naming it depended on memory pathways located inside the brain, rather than structures in the nose. In other words, they could still smell, but could no longer remember the identity of the particular odor.

Low levels of *acetylcholine*, the same chemical that transfers and stores memory, was linked to the loss of recognition of smells.

This meant that it was brain damage, not the loss of the ability to smell, that was responsible for the loss of ability to recognize smells. Odor tests are sometimes used in the diagnosis of Alzheimer's.

In our daily lives, odors affect us in many subtle ways. For example, there is mounting evidence that people choose their mates through the sense of smell. Chemicals called *pheremones* trigger interpersonal attraction. This chemical attraction is the origin of the saying that there is "chemistry" between people.

In a new study on pheremones, it was found that the human scents that people found most attractive were those that were the most chemically different than their own. In other words, the more the DNA of one person differed from another, the more attractive they found the other's smell. This fascinating finding is evidence that pheremones may not only contribute to sexual attraction, but may promote genetic diversity as well.

Recently it was discovered that smelling can actually improve memory. Dr. Brian Lyman of the Monell Chemical Senses Center in Philadelphia says putting something with a strong odor in a shirt pocket during studying, and using the same odor when taking a test increases the amount of information remembered.

A Yale University study showed that students who whiffed chocolate while studying remembered 21% of the words they had written down the day before compared to 14% for those in the control group. Researcher Frank Schab says that strong odors "piggy-back" other memories because the brain so easily remembers scent.

SKILL MEMORY

Also called *motor memory, procedural memory,* or *implicit memory,* skill memory is the ability to remember how to do things. Complex tasks such as walking, talking, playing a musical instrument, or riding a bicycle are all examples of skill memory. Skill memory is controlled by a specific area of the brain called the motor cortex.

Skill memory is unconscious and permanent. Amnesia victims may forget day-to-day events, but their skill memory usually remains intact. Loss of this kind of memory is a sure sign of serious brain deterioration.

Even if you haven't ridden a bike for several decades, you probably could get back on one and ride it with little effort But because skill memory is unconscious, even though you can ride the bike, you cannot tell someone how you do it. Skill memory records processes, not words.

Once a skill is learned, it is often difficult to unlearn. For example, when the transition from dial phones to touch tone phones took place in this country, many people found they had trouble remembering phone numbers. The change from manipulating a dial to pressing a series of buttons necessitated learning new patterns of movement, and new memories had to be recorded in order to recall the numbers.

Although skill memory involves recorded patterns of muscle movements, research has shown that the brain stores these programs in greater detail than just what muscles must be used.

For example, when you sign your name on a check, you use your hand and wrist muscles to move the pen. Although your signature is never exactly the same, it is remarkably similar each time you write it.

But it is also strikingly similar when you write it on a blackboard, even though you are now using your arm to make the movements your wrist made before. The memory program for your signature then must be more complex than just a pattern of muscle movements.

VISCERAL MEMORY

When I was fifteen years old, I worked in a gas station. It was my job to open the station in the morning, and to do this, I had to get up at 5 a.m. Half awake, I would start each day with a bowl of corn flakes. One day as I was eating breakfast in a semiconscious state, I spooned up a large cricket from my bowl.

In addition to jolting me into consciousness, this experience left me with a distaste for corn flakes that lasts to this day. The nauseating feeling I get when I look at corn flakes is a *visceral memory*.

Eating is a natural response to hunger, but visceral memories can, and do, interfere with this process. Some of our earliest memories focus around eating. The feeding experiences of infancy have a profound effect on adult behavior. For example, for some infants, the feeling of a full stomach is associated with pleasant feelings. While the infant is feeding, she is being held, cuddled, and soothed by the sound of Mother's voice.

When this child becomes an adult, she may attempt to reproduce these nurturing feelings by filling her stomach. This type of behavior can lead to compulsive eating. Conversely, a child who has had a history of unpleasant experiences eating may learn to avoid food, and find themselves eating only enough to survive.

Visceral memories are bundles of information about how internal organs function tied with pleasant or unpleasant experiences. The common term for visceral memory is *gut feelings*.

AUDITORY MEMORY

Auditory memory is the memory for sounds. It is this type of memory that enables us to recognize a friend's voice, a dog barking, or a bell ringing. Auditory memory is remarkably accurate. Many of us have learned to recognize a person just from the sound of their footsteps, the way they cough, sneeze, or how they clear their throat. This type of memory works so well that most of us never think about it.

Auditory memory also functions to record the *sequence* of sounds. It is in this way that we memorize songs. People with exceptionally good auditory memory often become accomplished musicians. Arturo Toscanini, one of the greatest conductors of all time, could remember the entire score of a symphony after hearing it only one or two times. Once he had committed a score to memory, he could write it down note-for-note forty years later.

Studies show that about 40% of us are predominantly auditory when it comes to memorizing. That is, we learn best when we hear something. People with auditory preference would much rather study by listening to a taped lecture than to read notes.

However, the majority of us, the other 60%, prefer to use visual memory. This is one reason why television is more popular than radio. We like to watch something related to the information we hear. Media researchers were surprised when they found that people prefer to see someone reading the news rather than merely hearing them on the radio.

VISUAL MEMORY

Visual memory is the ability to remember and recognize faces, places, and objects. The ability to remember faces is a very important survival mechanism. Thousands of years ago, when humans lived in huts and had to hunt for food, they needed to be able to recognize whether an approaching person was a friend or a stranger. Those that didn't do well at this didn't survive.

You know from your own experience that it's easier to remember a face than a name. In fact, you can memorize a face after seeing it for only a minute or two. We are a visually oriented species, and our visual memory is extremely accurate and permanent. You seldom hear of anyone trying to improve their visual memory.

The *occipital lobe*, a large area in the back of the brain, is devoted to the processing of visual material. Damage to this part of the brain results in a disorder called *prosopagnosia*. People with this disorder completely lose the ability to recognize faces, even their own.

SENSORY MEMORY AND LANGUAGE

The process of learning language begins with learning the names of objects. This is done by a parent pointing to an object and pronouncing its name. The child looks at the object and hears a sound uttered. To learn the name of an object, the child must first be able to form a mental image in visual memory. This mental image allows the child to recognize the object when he sees it again.

The next task is the tying of the mental picture to the word through the process of association. Once this association is formed, the child is able to call up the mental image just by hearing the word. You now have thousands of these image-word links stored in your memory.

Think of an elephant. A car. A dog. As you think of these words, mental pictures of the objects instantaneously appear in your mind. Later in this book, you are going to use this function of the brain to help you memorize new material.

INFORMATIONAL MEMORY

When we think of improving memory, we are usually referring to *informational* or *declarative* memory. Informational memory is the ability to recall facts and events, and this type of memory requires conscious effort.

Informational memory, unlike the other types of memory just mentioned, is not a survival mechanism, and therefore doesn't work nearly as well as the other types. Until a few centuries ago, our senses were much more vital to our survival than information, so the brain's declarative memory ability is not as reliable as sensory memory.

One of the secrets of improving memory, therefore, is to bypass informational memory, and memorize information using the types of memory that already work well—sensory memory. As we shall see, this is the basis of most memory improvement techniques

SEMANTIC MEMORY

One subcategory of informational memory is *semantic memory*. It is the memory of what words, gestures, signs, and cultural symbols mean to us.

Alzheimer's disease causes devastating memory damage, attacking and destroying the cells that store memories. But even in those with advanced stages of the disease, about half of Alzheimer's patients still retain a good portion of semantic memory.

WORKING MEMORY

The most recent memory research has focused on what scientists call *working memory*. It is working memory that enables us to hold part of a sentence in our minds until we get to the end. This factor of memory also allows us to keep several things in our minds simultaneously. It is also working memory that begins to slow down and falter between ages 40 and 50

EPISODIC MEMORY

Episodic memory is the storehouse of our personal past. It contains all memories of things gone by. Although most people will readily admit that they have faulty informational memory, they insist that their episodic memory is perfect. Many arguments originate from disputes about who did or said something.

But despite our steadfast conviction about our own memories, in reality, episodic memory is unquestionably the most unreliable.

We know from years of research that eyewitness accounts of past events are remarkably inaccurate. This in part is because episodic memory is not recalled, but recreated. Instead of accessing the information like a computer does, each time we remember something, we recreate a story about what we recall.

Depending on our mood, the situation, our own beliefs and opinions, and many other factors, this story is a little different each time we recount it. Over time, our recollection of an experience may cease to have any resemblance to what actually happened. In chapter four, we will discover some of the reasons that this is so.

CHAPTER THREE

THE MEMORY PROCESS

Just how does something become a memory? How does the experience of eating that great cheese sandwich you had last week get processed and stored, so that you can tell your ncighbor about it a week later?

Although researchers have been exploring this question for centuries, we still don't understand just how memories are formed. However, we do know that all information must go through a specific set of steps before it becomes a memory.

STIMULUS

All memory begins with *stimuli,* sources of information that are new to the mind. Most stimuli originate from the outside world. Every sight, sound, taste, touch and smell is a stimulus. But memories can also be generated internally by the brain itself, as happens during dreaming, fantasy, thought, creativity, and problem solving. In fact, all of our art, science, and creativity are the end product of generating, synthesizing, and re-membering newly formed internal ideas. Many groundbreaking inventions originated from remembering information that was originally generated in dreams.

RECEPTORS

In order for any external stimulus to be recorded as a memory, it must first be processed through the nervous system. Information coming from the outside world is picked up by the millions of specialized cells in the sense organs, called *receptors*. Your eyes, ears, mouth and skin all contain receptors.

Although we all process this information in the same manner, some of us have a preferred mode of processing information. For example, visually oriented people would rather watch something, while people with a preference for sound would rather hear it. This preference for a specific type of information comes from your particular set of stimulus filters.

STIMULUS FILTERS

Although we encounter millions of bits of information each day, we actually remember only a small portion of them. What we do remember is controlled by the mechanism of filtering. Like any filter, this mechanism eliminates unwanted material. Stimulus filters scan all incoming information, and allow into consciousness only the most important data.

Each of us inherits a unique set of stimulus filters. We are born with an array of natural talents and abilities that make it easy for us to remember certain types of information.

This is true in part because of individual differences in the hard wiring of the brain. Just as people differ in hair color, eye color, and height, each person's brain structure is unique. In the last few years, researchers have actually found physical differences in brain structure that correspond with different abilities and professions.

We all know people who have excellent memories for certain things. The word we use to describe our inborn abilities is *talent.*

For example, you probably know someone with a natural ability to remember music. She can remember a song after hearing it only once. On the other hand, those born without this ability to process music, a quality sometimes called *tone deafness*, cannot remember a song even after hearing it fifty times. (Then there are those with no musical ability that think they have it. The term we use for this is *painfully annoying.*)

So while some people excel in certain types of memory, others suffer specific deficits. These people are said to have *learning disabilities.* People with learning disabilities may be unable to process certain types of information, and therefore they cannot store it. This deficit in storage has often been mistaken for a memory problem, but it's actually a filtering problem.

In addition to inheriting stimulus filters, we form them as a result of experience. For example, if you had a history teacher that made history exciting and interesting, you'd find it easy to remember important historical events and figures. You would develop an emotional investment in history, and enjoy being able to recall this type of information.

But if your history class was dull and boring, you would learn to feel that way about history in general, and find that historical information slips through your memory like water through a sieve. If you failed history, you would find that from that time on you would automatically tune out historical subjects, and not pay attention to information that has anything to do with history. Your filters would shut out anything that remotely resembled history.

In other words, we all associate emotions with information, and if the emotions are unpleasant, we'll avoid similar information in the future. Psychologists call this emotional avoidance a *mental block.*

It's natural to spend more time doing what we do well, because it makes us feel good. Because our stimulus filters determine what kinds of information we process, they guide our lives. A person may use his musical ability to become a composer. And one born with natural mathematical ability may use it to become a scientist.

It is filtering then that steers us away from what we are not interested in, and draws us toward what pleases us.

Many of you have noticed this filtering process in your children. For example, if you tell a child, "The cookies are upstairs on the second shelf, and take out the trash before you leave for school," you know that they are more likely to remember where the cookies are than to take the trash out.

As adults, we continue to selectively attend to things from the world, storing those things that interest us, and filtering out the things that don't.

In reality, much of what we think of as forgetting is actually the result of filtering out what we don't care to remember.

THE ORIENTING RESPONSE

The process by which our stimulus filters select what is to be attended to is called the *orienting response*. Orienting is an automatic, unconscious process. It is active even when you are sleeping. It is this reflex that allows a new mother to sleep through the noise of a police siren, only to be awakened a moment later by a slight whimper from her newborn.

While having a conversation with someone in a room full of people, we automatically focus on what the other person is saying. Without effort, all other conversations are filtered out. But if someone across the room calls our name, the orienting response refocuses our attention, and we turn our heads to see who called us. This type of selective listening is called the *cocktail party phenomenon*.

The orienting response is an automatic mechanism that tells us what to pay attention to at any given moment. Because we are not consciously aware of this, our attention is often diverted even when we wish it to be on the task before us. Have you ever gotten up out of your chair fully intending to do something, only to be distracted a moment later? This is the orienting response at work. When something catches our attention, we forget our previous intent.

Many things that we say we don't remember are actually never stored in our memories at all, because the orienting response placed our attention elsewhere at the time of the event.

SHORT TERM MEMORY

Once a piece of information has been selected by the orienting response, and passed through the stimulus filter for processing, it enters *short-term memory*.

Short-term memory holds only a small amount of information, and holds this information for a very brief period of time; about twenty or thirty seconds.

You've probably had the experience of looking up a number in a phone book, walking over to the phone, dialing part of the number, and suddenly realizing that you have forgotten the rest of it.

What do you do? You look the number up again, and this time say the number over and over to yourself until you reach the phone. If you're successful in dialing the number, you finish your conversation, and hang up. But if you have to call again in a few minutes, you find you have once more forgotten the number.

This happens because information stays in short-term

memory for only a few seconds unless it is rehearsed. You must repeat the phone number to yourself in order to keep it active in short term memory.

Short-term memory holds only enough information to store about one phone number. It's impossible to look up three or four phone numbers, and remember them long enough to dial them.

If you use a number every day, however, eventually you find that you know the number without having to look it up again. The number has now been stored in the next stage of memory—long-term memory.

LONG TERM MEMORY

In 1890, William James distinguished between two types of memory which he called *primary memory,* now called short-term memory, and *secondary memory*, which lasts for an extended period of time (now called long term memory.) But it wasn't until 1958 that the terms short-term and long-term memory were coined by Broadbent.

Broadbent found that unlike short-term memory, long-term memory stored information in a relatively permanent fashion. It also has the capacity to hold large amounts of data—as far as we know, no one has ever come close to filling up their long term memory.

RETRIEVAL AND RECOLLECTION

The final stage in the memory process is the ability to retrieve the stored information. It is the ability or inability to access information that is the focus of most memory research.

In reality, however, most of the time the inability to remember something is caused by a failure in the storage process just described. The most common cause of not remembering is the simple failure of information being transferred from short-term to long-term memory.

One way to store information in your long-term memory is to rehearse it many times and review it frequently. This sends a message to your memory that the information is important and should be stored.

There are occasions however, that something can be stored in long-term memory without rehearsal. If you are extremely interested in something, you may store it after hearing or seeing it only once. Also, events that are unusual or emotionally arousing, such as the plot of a good book or movie, may be stored after only one exposure.

FLASHBULB MEMORY

One morning I was walking up the stairs in my health club when I saw an amazing sight on the television in the lounge. It was a picture of the space shuttle *Challenger* exploding. This disaster killed seven people, and brought the entire space program to its knees.

Although this happened years ago, I still have a vivid memory of walking up those stairs and seeing the ship explode. As you read this paragraph, you too may recall where you were and what you were doing when you heard this tragic news.

Scientists call this type of memory a *flashbulb memory*. The emotional impact of these memories drive them immediately into long-term memory. Memories that are stored in this manner tend to last a lifetime.

Flashbulb memory seems incredibly accurate, but is it? Research shows that flashbulb memories select certain elements of an experience for storage, and edit out other components. For example, although I recall the picture of the exploding *Chal-*

lenger quite vividly, I don't remember what day of the week it was, or even what year it was.

Even though flashbulb memories seem so vivid and accurate, they actually change with time.

The day after the space shuttle *Challenger* burst apart, psychologist Ulric Neisser asked his students to write a description of where they were and exactly what they were doing when they heard the news of the disaster. Three years later, he contacted the students and asked them to recall the same experience. Over one third of the students wrote descriptions that were totally unrelated to their original description!

What impressed Neisser the most, however, was that the students were absolutely convinced that their memories were accurate. When shown their original written descriptions of the event, some of them actually claimed that someone else must have copied their handwriting, and written the original account!

EMOTION AND MEMORY

If you look back in your life right now, you will find that much of what you remember were emotionally arousing instances, or important events such as graduating, getting married, or getting a promotion.

Most people remember the last time they rode a roller coaster better then what they had to eat last week because roller coaster rides are more emotionally arousing events than meals.

Even relatively unemotional events, however, are filtered through our emotional brains before they are stored. For example, the words *velvet* and *granite* each have an emotional component. You would probably rather run your hand over a piece of velvet than a piece of granite. The words *pudding* and *blood* carry emotional components also. Given the choice, you probably would rather put your hand in a bowl of pudding than a pool of blood.

While you might not have enjoyed what you just read, the emotion attached to the previous sentence increased the probability that you will remember it. If no emotion at all is attached to an event, it will not be remembered at all.

It appears that emotions affect memory in several ways:

- **First, exciting and interesting information is stored with less effort than dull and boring information,** because emotion increases our arousal. We call this emotional investment *attention*.

- **Second, the emotions experienced along with information determine whether we pay attention to similar information in the future.** This makes it easy for us to remember the things we enjoy. We call this experience *developing an interest*.

- **Third, the mood that you are in when you learn something has an effect on your ability to remember it later.** This is why people remember every bad thing their spouse has done when they get angry at them. This quality of memory is called *state dependent memory* (which is discussed later in this book).

Finally, although emotion does help us remember, research has shown us that regardless of how strongly we feel about a memory, it may be completely incorrect.

CHAPTER FOUR

WHY WE FORGET

It seems that everybody worries about their memory. But because we've all been taught that memory gets worse with age, it's no surprise that as we get older, we become anxious every time we forget something. Every lost pair of sunglasses or keys, every misplaced pen or forgotten promise, is seen as evidence that we are getting senile.

But actually, memory doesn't get significantly worse with age. The truth is that memory is always bad. If you think about it for a minute, you'll see this is true. If you have reared children, you know that their memories are terrible. Kids lose everything—their shoes, their jackets, their homework. They forget what you tell them. They forget to do their chores, they forget everything. But they have something that you don't have. They have parents in the house to remind them of things.

It's not surprising then that we continue to forget things as we get older. But things haven't changed, we just notice it more.

Now certain conditions such as nutritional deficiencies and disorders like Alzheimer's disease do cause significant memory loss. But barring this, our memory at seventy can remain almost as sharp as it was at seven.

Even though this is true, we still forget a great number of the events in our lives. Certain experiences disappear forever. Why do we forget so much of what we experience?

Actually, the human mind is a forgetting machine. It is built to forget. To understand this, let's look at the way memory works in non-humans.

The more complicated an animal's nervous system is, the more easily it forgets. Insects have a very limited ability to learn new behavior. Everything that they need know is programmed into them at birth. They come into the world completely equipped for survival, and they don't forget anything. But they are also incapable of learning. They cannot modify their behavior.

Birds and other animals with more complicated nervous systems are more adaptable. They are still very well equipped with the knowledge they need to survive from birth, but they have to learn some of their life skills from their parents. For example, birds are genetically programmed to sing, but they must learn the correct mating song from their parents.

But humans need to be taught everything they need to know to survive, and consequently, we must have a much larger capacity for storing memory. We also have a much greater ability to forget. Our ability to discard unwanted information allows us to adapt to new environments, developing and changing as our surroundings change. We erase old behaviors and learn new skills that help us adapt. As we change, we forget what we no longer need

In the previous chapter we learned that memory is step-wise process. Each step is essential for the storage and recovery

Here is an exercise of two parts. Each part will make points about different aspects of memory.

Part One

Go back in time ten years. Think about that year in your life. Now tell a friend everything you can remember about that period.

You probably noticed several things:

- First, you will probably remember very little about that year.
- It probably took you only a few minutes to recount everything you remember.
- What you did remember probably consisted of high and low points in your life.

This shows that we soon forget much of what we do. Emotionally important events are remembered more readily.

Part Two

For this second part, you'll need to grab your high school yearbook. Before you glance through it, begin this section of the exercise.

- Name every person you remember from high school. Take your time and list them all.

- Now open your yearbook and look through it. See how many people you still remember but were unable to recall.

This demonstrates the difference between recall and recognition memory. External clues often jog memory better than internal ones.

of memory. Therefore, if any one step fails, memory is not stored. Let's examine how problems in each step impede memory.

STIMULUS PROBLEMS

As mentioned in chapter three, all memory begins with a stimulus. A stimulus might be a sight, sound, taste or smell, or even a complicated and delicate pattern of motion such as the graceful and beautiful movements of a ballet dancer, accomplished through the memorization of hundreds of separate movements.

For any stimulus to be picked up by the nervous system, it must be strong enough to trigger the receptor. Scientists call this minimum intensity the *stimulus threshold*. A mosquito is often able to land on the body, puncture the skin, and leave without our awareness because its delicate touch is below the stimulus threshold of the touch receptors in our skin. We only become aware of the insect's visit because of the itching caused by the bite.

In the 1950's, several movie theaters reported that they sold more popcorn and soda because of hidden messages flashed on the screen saying "eat popcorn" and "drink Coke." The publicity generated from this experiment launched an entire industry based what came to be known as *subliminal learning*. Since that time, millions of dollars have been spent on subliminal tapes that claim to help break habits, increase self esteem, and boost productivity.

However, not one study done since the 1950 movie experiment has shown that anything can be learned subliminally. It appears that sounds that are too quiet to be heard are not registered or processed by the brain. So, unfortunately, subliminal tapes do not work.

To be discernable, information must also have low signal to noise ratios. This means that the information you are trying to learn should be clear and uncontaminated. This is why teachers insist that students remain quiet during class time. Too much noise makes concentration difficult.

On the other hand, too little stimulation can also lead to memory problems. It is common for people to become less active as they grow older. Older people are less physically active, less socially active, and seek out less stimulation.

Many elderly people do very little each day but sit and watch television. They are chronically under-stimulated. These lonely and forgotten people are seldom spoken to, seldom touched, and rarely encouraged to engage in social activity. This chronic loss of stimulation greatly accelerates memory loss. I've seen high functioning people deteriorate within weeks after they are placed in a nursing home where no stimulation is offered.

It could be said that under-stimulation is literally the hobgoblin of little minds. An under-stimulated brain eventually begins to atrophy, shrink, and deteriorate.

In fact, chronic under-stimulation can lead to Hallucinations. The brain needs a certain amount of stimulation to function properly, and if it cannot get it from the environment, it will manufacture it. Experiments in sensory deprivation show that deprived of external events, the brain will begin to generate stimuli within a few hours.

Conversely, stimulating a brain with new experiences and novel environments actually causes neurons to grow new connections. In short, stimulation helps a brain stay healthy. The bottom line is, the more active you remain, the better your memory will function.

RECEPTOR PROBLEMS

Many years ago, children who were hard of hearing were classified as retarded. They were often shunned by society and considered unteachable. Eventually it was discovered that deaf children were just as capable of learning and remembering as anyone—they simply had a receptor problem.

As we age, our receptors begin to falter. Eyes and ears no longer function as well as they once did. This decrease in function is usually slow and insidious, and may not be noticed for a considerable time.

As hearing begins to fail, people often complain that others are not speaking clearly or loudly enough. Many people deny that they have a hearing problem even when it is apparent to others around them. Of course, when hearing fails, auditory memory suffers also. What can't be heard cannot be remembered. For this reason, some people begin to complain of memory problems when what is actually happening is a loss of the ability to detect sound.

It's important to be aware that many older people also lose much of their ability to smell and taste. This often results in a decrease in the pleasure of eating. When eating decreases, malnutrition may occur, which, as we will see later, can have a profound effect on memory.

FILTERING PROBLEMS

Can you imagine what it might be like to remember everything? To remember every meal you've ever eaten? Every cut and bruise you've ever had? Every disappointment and loss you've ever experienced? This would crowd our minds with drivel, and make our lives miserable. The truth is that much of what we do each day is better off forgotten. Repetitive, day-to-day tasks and uninteresting experiences are soon forgotten because remembering them serves no useful purpose. Much of what we experience never enters memory at all, because our filters see it as unimportant. But when filters break down, memory suffers.

STRESS

Some memory experts believe that stress is one of the major causes of forgetting. In general, the more stress that you are under, the more poorly your memory will work.

One of the reasons for this is that stress causes stimulus filters to break down. When filters break down, nothing in the environment gets filtered out.

You have probably noticed that when you're feeling stressed, every little thing bothers you. Friends bother you, kids bother you, your husband or wife bothers you—every pop, crack, and door slam makes you jump.

This causes stimulus *overload*. Short-term memory can't handle this much input. When this happens, you find you can't pay attention to anything, and therefore you are unable to transfer the information into long-term memory.

The net result is that short-term memory stops processing new information. Later on, when the stress is over, you find that you can't remember much of anything that went on during the time that you were stressed.

When people start feeling stressed, they instinctively try to get away from the noise and distraction they can no longer filter. They attempt to "get away from it all" by taking a vacation.

Stress also makes it more difficult to remember things that you already know. When you are stressed, you find that your mind is filled with concerns about the fact that you are under pressure, and this preoccupation interferes with your ability to recall information (state dependence, which is discussed below, is also partially responsible for this lack of recall.)

Even worse, several studies suggest that stress is one of the causes of brain-cell death. Chemicals called *free radicals* which increase during stress, can actually destroy cells in the amygdala and hippocampus.

Robert Sapolski at Stanford University has spent several years undertaking studies that suggest that a family of hormones called *glucocorticoids* can kill brain cells. These hormones are designed to mobilize glucose during the fight or flight response, but repeated stress overloads cells in the hippocampus with these substances, and kills them.

The hippocampus is the part of the brain that is responsible for the transfer of short-term memory to long term memory.

It has been estimated that as we age we lose from 10 to 40% of our hippocampal cells. Memory impairment begins when about 15% of the cells are lost. According to Sapolski, stress can kill these cells.

It is not catastrophe, but the cumulative effect of everyday stressful events that leads to this deterioration. Therefore, Sapolski suggests, the best method of prevention is to learn coping skills and stress reduction techniques.

WORRY

Still another reason that certain items are forgotten has come to be known as the *Ziegarnick Effect,* named after the researcher who studied it. Zeigarnick gave subjects twenty simple tasks that each took only a few minutes. She interrupted the subjects during half of the tasks, and did not allow them to complete them. When the subjects were done, they were asked to recall as many of the tasks as possible.

She found that 68% of the uncompleted tasks were recalled as opposed to 43% of the completed ones. The Zeigarnick effect then is the propensity to recall uncompleted tasks more easily than completed tasks.

In part, this is useful. The effect makes it more likely that you will remember chores that have not been completed than ones that have been finished. For example, if I ask you to think about your bills, do you think about the ones that you have paid, or the ones that you haven't paid? The Zeigarnick effect helps you focus on what must be done, rather than what you have done.

On the down side, however, unfinished business tends to stay on your mind and fill your consciousness. The popular term for this is *worry*.

Beyond question, worry interferes with concentration. It fills your mind so full of the flotsam of unfinished business and unresolved conflict that nothing else is allowed to enter.

In addition, people who worry become so filled with anxiety that stimulus filters break down, and we've already seen that filter malfunction means memory loss.

Here is a five step method for reducing worry:

1.Write down all of your worries.

2.After you have completed the list, read it over and **decide which items on your list are within your power to change.**

3.Write a plan of action for facing these challenges, and commit yourself to a time and place to resolve them.

4.Let go of the worries that you have no power to change. Thinking about them is a waste of time.

5.If you still feel that you need "worry time," set aside 15-30 minutes a day to do nothing but worry. When that time is over, enjoy yourself.

OVERLOAD

Overload occurs when information is coming in at too rapid a rate. What happens is tha. the new data "bumps out" the information already stored in your short-term memory, and prevents it from moving on to be warehoused in long-term memory. Effectively your memory system goes on strike. This is why we find ourselves saying, "Whoa, slow down!" when someone is giving us too much too fast.

The best way to avoid overload is to take information in at the rate in which you can process it. If someone is giving you too much information to quickly, it is perfectly proper to ask them to slow down.

INTERFERENCE

When information comes in from several sources at once, only a small portion of it is allowed into short-term memory. As we have seen, stimulus filters block out all but the most important and interesting data. This is why it's not a good idea to study while listening to the radio or when watching your favorite television show.

As mentioned earlier, the older we get, the more sensitive we become to the disruption of interference. Our ability to filter becomes impaired. Therefore, the older you are the more it becomes necessary to keep unnecessary input at a minimum.

Research has shown that you can increase your ability to remember something if you review it right before going to bed at night. This is because the information is the last thing you see before you fall asleep. No other information competes with it.

This allows the information to be stored in long-term memory during your slumber (a topic that is further explored in chapter 11).

Exercise: Picturing a Penny

Here is an exercise based on research by Adams and Nickerson which will illustrate how the stimulus filters block information that is deemed insignificant. This exercise may have you searching for a penny to check the right answers, but don't peek until you've reached the end.

- Without looking, draw a picture of the face side of a Lincoln-head penny.
- Which way is the former president facing?
- What words hover above him?
- What words or information appear on either side of him?

You may be surprised to find that although you have looked at these copper-colored coins thousands of times, you have some doubts about what is really on them. The reason you're unsure is that you never considered this information important, and therefore you never stored it.

Okay, it's alright to check your answers against a penny now.

STORAGE FAILURE

Because we do not have to remember everything to survive, we filter out what does not interest us, or that we don't consider important. This again is a function of our stimulus filters and our emotions.

Of course, any item that is filtered out does not get stored in long-term memory. If you are asked to remember it, you find that you can't. This is not because your memory is bad, but because you never stored the information in the first place.

An experience that is not stored in long term memory is not an experience at all. In fact, you have no knowledge that it ever happened. When someone suggests that you did or said something that you have not stored, you will deny it with complete conviction.

Have you ever picked up a valuable object, put it away, and then completely forgot where you put it? This is storage failure at its worst!

LACK OF USE

A phenomenon that scientists call *passive decay* suggests that unused memories become less available to us as time passes by.

For example, you may call a good friend on a regular basis. Because you call her a lot, you find it easy to remember her telephone number. However, if she moves to a different town, and changes her phone number, you've got to learn the new number. Over time, you forget the original number because you no longer use it.

As time passes we forget much of what we learn because of the process of passive decay. Many of us at some time during our school years, were required to memorize the names of the presidents, or the names of all the states and their capitals. How many of them can you remember now? Unless you used a memory system to store these things, you've lost this information through passive decay.

Memory researchers have found some evidence that this process may be caused by the actual dissolving of old connections between neurons in order to make new ones, much in the same way that an old building is torn down to make room for a new one. It seems that memory is constantly under construction.

Have you ever known someone who tells you the same stories again and again? The reason is that this is what they remember about their life, and they remember it because they have told the story so frequently. As they have done, you can prevent passive decay by rehearsing important information frequently. In this way the information stays at the threshold of consciousness.

REPRESSION

Simply put, repression is the process of avoiding unpleasant memories. It is an automatic forgetting mechanism that allows us to ignore things that don't agree with our self-image.

This process sometimes spawns arguments, when someone accuses you of having done or said something, and you vehemently deny ever having done it.

Even though you may not remember these things, the emotional component of the memories are not forgotten. And these emotions affect your ability to record new information about yourself.

For example, if you see yourself as an intelligent, sensitive, emotionally mature individual, you tend to repress every stupid, insensitive, immature thing that you have done.

Conversely, if you see yourself as an incompetent fool, you will repress all the intelligent and successful things you have done, and remember your blunders.

Unpleasant emotions cause you to avoid situations that you remember as painful. Therefore, you may shy away from learning something because of the anticipated pain.

Some fears and phobias may be caused by repressed experiences. There is evidence, for example, that some agoraphobics lost a parent or loved one during their childhood. The forgotten trauma of the loss later manifests itself in panic attacks whenever the traumatized person is away from a loved one. Often, when this is pointed out, the phobia goes away.

Contrary to popular belief, repression does not wipe out memories of trauma, or erase entire sections of a person's life.

Research suggests that the repression of painful memories is actually caused by the avoidance of thinking about them, not by an active process called repression. The human mind does not hide memories from itself.

The rash of "repressed memory therapies" that exist today are based on the false assumption that abuse memories can be pushed into the unconscious, and that therapy and hypnosis can "de-repress" them. This is absolutely untrue. There is simply no method known to science to recover a lost memory.

MOTIVATED FORGETTING

Have you ever forgotten a dentist appointment, a promise, or someone's birthday? If so you may have experienced motivated forgetting. This type of forgetting is based on the desire to forget. Motivated forgetting involves pushing hurt, anger, or fear into the unconscious. These emotions are then dealt with by forgetting material related to them.

This differs from *intentional forgetting*, where there is a deliberate effort not to remember. Motivated forgetting happens "by accident." The desire to forget is not focused or conscious. This process always involves a negative emotion that has not been acknowledged.

If this concept is difficult to understand, it may help to think about it in terms of motivation to remember. For example, when I was discussing this problem in one of my memory seminars, a student interrupted me and said, "Wait a minute. I forgot to go to my best friend's birthday party a few months ago. I love this person. Are you telling me I deliberately forgot?"

My anser was "Yes". Now, imagine that one of your friends called you and said, "My birthday party is next Tuesday at three o'clock. If you will be there at three, I will give you a cashier's check for $100,000." Do you think you would forget this party? In this case you would be highly motivated to remember.

The things that you forget can be things you decided not to remember. My student may have forgotten the party because she unconsciously decided to dismiss it from her mind. This may have been because of some unconscious hurt or anger towards her friend. She may have avoided discussing this feeling because of fear of hurting her friend, or because of guilt about being angry at someone she obviously loved.

This type of forgetting has been referred to as having a *mental block*. One patient of mine forgot his wedding anniversary several years in a row. When he was able to recognize and resolve his anger toward his wife, his memory immediately improved.

INTENTIONAL FORGETTING

Yet another cause of forgetting unpleasant memories is a similar process called *intentional forgetting*. This is similar to repression, except that it is deliberately controlled. When you have been hurt emotionally or when you have done something embarrassing, you often try not to think about it. This helps you to forget the incident. Sometimes you do this by forcing yourself to think of something else. This helps you to forget by preventing you from rehearsing the memory, which then allows it to fade through passive decay.

Psychologists suggest that an effective way to forget something is through a process called *thought stopping*. This involves yelling "Stop!" whenever you notice yourself thinking an unwanted thought. The emotional intrusion of yelling "stop" prevents the thought from being rehearsed.

The differences between repression, motivated forgetting and intentional forgetting are subtle and unclear. The defining differences involve the automatic nature of repression, the lack of awareness in motivated forgetting, and the deliberate, conscious effort of intentional forgetting.

However, regardless of how the process takes place, the results are always the same—that which is not thought about is eventually forgotten.

RETRIEVAL FAILURE

Most of us have experienced retrieval failure as the "tip -of-the-tongue" phenomenon— that uncanny feeling of knowing that you know something, but not being able to recall it.

This phenomenon shows us that memory retrieval is not an all-or-nothing process. For example, you may see a picture of an actor, and be able to recall the titles of several of their movies, but not their name. Or you may be able to say what letter his name begins with, but not remember the name itself.

This suggests that memory is stored in many different categories, and that each memory may be stored in segments which are distributed in many locations in our brains. We may be able to retrieve one segment, while the other pieces elude us.

It also illustrates that there is a difference between *availability* and *accessibility* of information—you may know that you have the information available, you know that you know it, but you just can't seem to make it available to yourself at the time you want it.

This phenomenon also tells us that retrieval of infor-mation is not always a conscious process. You know from your own experience that when you encounter a tip-of-the-tongue episode, if you stop trying to remember and go on about your business, the desired information eventually pops into your head. While psychologists still do not fully understand what causes retrieval failure, one possible reason for it is a process called state dependence.

STATE DEPENDENCE

State dependence is the process of associating emotions, moods, and surroundings with the things that you remember. This means that if you were in a bad mood when you learned something, you will recall it best the next time that you're grumpy. If you were happy when you studied something, you will recall it best the next time that you're feeling cheerful.

If you think about this for a while, you will see how this principle works in your own life. When you are furious at a friend, don't you find it easy to remember everything that they have ever done wrong? When you are feeling anxious, don't you find it extemely easy to find things to worry about? When you are depressed, doesn't the world seem to be full of troubles? And when you are feeling good, doesn't the world seem full of great and inspiring things?

Many students have noticed that the minute they leave a classroom, all of the answers they couldn't remember popped back into their heads. If this has ever happened to you, you may have said to yourself, "Why couldn't I answer that question? I knew the answer all along!"

The anxiety you felt while taking a test put you in a different state of mind. When you left the room you became more relaxed, which was most likely the state that you were in when you learned the information in the first place.

How many times have you gotten up out of your chair to go do something, only to find yourself standing in the middle of the kitchen without the slightest idea of what you are doing there? Besides feeling very foolish, what did you do when this happened? If you're like most people, you returned to where you started. As you sat down, you immediately remembered why you got up.

When you were seated again, you recreated the state dependent variables under which the thought occurred to you, and this helped you to remember it.

Understanding state dependence can assist you in improving your ability to remember. For example, you can improve your ability to recall test answers if you learn to relax while studying, and to remain calm when you take a test.

You will also increase your ability to remember answers if you take state dependent variables into account when you study. This means becoming aware of what you do while you are studying. It is not a good idea to smoke, drink, or eat, or take any kind of medication while you are studying unless you intend to do the same thing when you take the exam, because all of these things become state dependent variables. (State dependent variables are discussed further in chapter 6.)

DISTORTION

Because of our differing individual stimulus filters, we do not see things accurately, but distort them through the lens of our expectations, prejudices, and beliefs. This causes us to modify what actually took place.

Attorneys are very aware of this phenomenon when it involves eyewitness testimony. They try to get as many witnesses as they can, because they know that several people seeing the same event will have different interpretations of what they saw.

In addition to this immediate distortion, scientists have found that memory is not as permanent and immutable as they once thought.

As time passes, memories distort and change radically. This process can cause us to remember something the way we wanted it to be rather than the way it really happened. It can cause us to omit certain facts from a memory and include others, and it can cause us to remember things that never really happened at all.

Have you ever had an argument with someone because you remember them saying something, and they deny saying it? Usually in these cases, the discussion elevates into a shouting match about who was right, and nothing ever gets settled. Both of you insist that you remember things correctly. What has actually happened is that both of you recalled the stored information to the best of your ability, but distortion caused your mind to record things the way that you wanted them to be, rather than the way that they actually occurred.

LACK OF CUES

A memory occurs when it is triggered by a cue. For example, if someone begins to talk to you about an old friend, hearing his name triggers memories about your experiences with him.

In everyday language, cues are often called reminders. The string tied around a finger is a popular image of this. A cue might be thought of as a hook that a memory hangs on. For this reason, memories that have many hooks are more easily retrieved than those that have only a few.

If the friend being discussed is a lifelong friend, there may be hundreds of cues that trigger memories about him. But if you only met him a week ago, these cues are few, and memory may be faulty. Of course, this means that the more cues you can attach to a piece of information, the easier it is to remember, and that is one of the cornerstones to memory improvement.

Exercise: Beginnings and endings

Memory stores information in categories, and tags each item with cues. Here's an exercise that demonstrates how important cues are.

Name the following items that begin with the letter shown:

a flower   P_____
a vegetable   T_____
a girl's name   T_____
a metal   T_____

Name the following items that end with the letter shown.

a flower   _____T
a vegetable   _____S
a girl's name   _____N
a metal   _____R

You probably discovered that the first letter of a word is a much more potent cue than the last letter.

In this chapter we have explored the ways that a normal healthy brain forgets. In the next chapter, we will look at some more serious memory problems.

CHAPTER FIVE

DEMENTIA

The word *dementia* literally means to lose one's mind (*de* meaning away from, and *ment* meaning mind). It is a word used to describe a variety of brain disorders that affect memory. Senility—the word that usually comes to mind when we feel our memory faltering—is derived from the Latin term *senex*, and literally means *old age*. The term *senile dementia* is based on the observation that many older people have memory problems.

Although most memory problems are not cause by dementing illness, some of them are. Without intervention, some of us are destined to suffer from dementia.

It is estimated that 1% of the population between the ages of 65 and 74 suffer from some type of dementia, while about 7% of those from 75 to 84, and 25% of people over 85 are afflicted. Currently about 2 million people in the U.S. suffer from severe dementia, while another 5 million have mild to moderate dementia.

Dementia is characterized by multiple problems in cognitive abilities without the loss of alertness. (Loss of alertness is called *delirium*).

Dementia is caused by a *brain damage*, and the parts of the brain that are most often harmed are the association areas in

47

the cerebral cortex. These sections of the brain integrate sensory information, thought, and purposeful behavior. When damage to this area occurs, both the outer and inner world become chaotic.

There are actually over sixty disorders that cause dementia, but Alzheimer's Disease,(often referred to as Dementia of the Alzheimer Type, or DAT) accounts for over half of all dementias in this country. Vascular disease, called Multi-Infarct Dementia accounts for another 20%. Brain tumors, infections, toxins, nutritional deficiencies, over-medication, metabolic problems, and other neurological disorders can also cause dementia-like symptoms.

SYMPTOMS OF DEMENTIA

Dementia is an exceptionally cruel and heartbreaking disease. The first warning signs are usually subtle changes in memory. The person may begin to have mild difficulties with short-term memory—what is experienced is almost immediately forgotten.

They may begin to have frequent problems with word finding, and new places and new social situations often become stressful and overwhelming. Because of this, the person may become more and more locked into a strict routine.

The victim may begin to have difficulty making simple decisions. Learning new information, calculating, making decisions and handling personal finances eventually become impossible. In addition, controlling emotions becomes more and more difficult, and the sufferer may have sudden, uncontrolled outbursts of anger or sadness.

Gradually confusion and memory loss increase. Even though the memory of past events may be maintained for a long time, simple tasks that have been performed for years are eventually forgotten. As memory continues to deteriorate, the treasured memories of the past are forgotten as well, and the person may no longer remember that they are married, or that they have children.

Eventually the person begins to have problems understanding what is said to them. As language function deteriorates, they also begin to have trouble making themselves understood.

Despite these losses, the person with dementia does not lose the ability to hear, respond to emotion, and be aware of touch. Even though these things are still perceived, they may cause confusion and agitation. Because the afflicted person is constantly attempting to cope with this confusion, he may engage in behaviors that have no external link to the environment.

As the person loses his grip on reality, he also becomes irritable, and may become verbally and physically aggressive. As the disease progresses, screaming, wandering aimlessly, and combative behaviors appear. In the later stages the individual might lose the ability to walk or stand up, and the ability to communicate in any meaningful way.

As the symptoms progress there is a loss of what health care providers call *activities of daily living* (ADL). About 9% of 65 to 75 year olds suffering from dementia need assistance with ADL, while about 45% of those over 85 need help.

MULTI-INFARCT DEMENTIA

As mentioned above, *dementia* means losing one's mind. An *infarct* is the closure of a blood vessel. Multi-infarct dementia (MID) then, means damage to the mind as a result of multiple episodes of interrupted blood flow to the brain.

Most doctors agree that multi-infarct dementia is caused by atherosclerosis of the blood vessels outside of the brain that supply it with blood—the carotid artery and the basilar artery.

The small blood vessels and capillaries in the brain itself may be fine, but the major blood vessels have blockages, or there can be abnormalities in the lining of the heart. Small clots (called *emboli*) break off from these areas and travel to the small vessels, where they get stuck, block the vessel, and cause a small stroke. Doing an ultrasound scan of the carotids and the heart can determine from where the clots originate.

Unlike Alzheimer's, where symptoms develop slowly, multi-infarct dementia symptoms come on suddenly, and with a highly unpredictable course.

This disorder can sometimes be brought on by a traumatic event such as the death of a spouse, or may occur after serious illness or after a delayed recovery from surgery. Most people with multi infarct dementia have a history of *transient ischemic attacks* (which are discussed in chapter 12 of this book) and high blood pressure (which is discussed in chapter 13). The symptoms of MID usually peak between the ages 40 and 60.

A common treatment of multi-infarct dementia is to use *vasodilators*, which are drugs that dilate the blood vessels. Two of these drugs, *Vasodilan* or *Arlidin*, are called *cerebral vasodilators*, which means that they dilate the blood vessels in the brain. The difficulty in using these drugs is that if the person has hardening of the arteries in the brain, the arteries are not flexible. Because these drugs are vasodilators, they dilate the arteries in parts of the body that are flexible, and can actually *decrease* blood flow to the brain. This makes the problems worse.

Hydergine, a drug manufactured by the Sandoz pharmaceutical company, is the most popular cerebral vasodilator. It has been shown to increase mental function in many patients who do not suffer solely from MID. This drug is under-utilized in the United States.

ALZHEIMER'S DISEASE

Of all memory disorders, there is none so well-known as Alzheimer's Disease. Alzheimer's is a progressive, degenerative disease of the brain, and although most of the people affected are over 65, Alzheimer's sometimes develops at a much younger age. The older one gets, the higher the risk of Alzheimer's— approximately 45% of people over 85 show symptoms.

Alzheimer's is the fourth leading cause of death among adults in the United States. Four million Americans currently suffer from the disease. The families of the victims spend over a hundred billion dollars each year caring for their afflicted loved ones. Barring any progress in combating the disease, there will be 14 million victims by the middle of the next century.

CAUSES

No one knows for certain just what causes Alzheimer's, but the disease always includes atrophy of the outer layer of the brain (called the *cortex*), neuron loss, and knotted bundles of tissue called *neurofibrillary tangles*. The primary neurological defect in the disease involves reduced activity of an enzyme called *choline-acetyl-transferase*, which causes lowered levels of the neurotransmitter *acetylcholine,* but there is also evidence of deficiencies in the neurotransmitters *dopamine* and *serotonin.*

Cell death is most rapid in the *amygdala* and the *hippocampus,* two parts of the brain discussed in chapter 1. Tragically, these are the areas of the brain most important for the processing of memory. The next sections to deteriorate are cortical areas on the brains outer surface. Eventually the frontal lobes, the part of the brain that regulates personality, are damaged. Once this happens, the person may become agitated and impulsive, and may have to be hospitalized. The time between the first symptoms and eventual death may be as long as twenty years.

In 1991, suspicions were confirmed that a fragment of protein called *beta-amyloid* is responsible for early onset Alzheimer's. When researcher Bruce Yankner injected beta-amyloid into the brains of rats, he found that the protein destroyed the same areas of the brain that Alzheimer's does.

The beta-amyloid molecule is actually a broken piece of a longer protein called APP. This complex protein begins producing beta-amyloid because of an error in the genetic code. There are 770 amino acids in APP, and in early onset Alzheimer's, it appears that the 717th amino acid is the wrong type.

Dr. John Hardy and his research team found that this genetic mistake was present in members of two families afflicted with early onset Alzheimer's. Family members with the gene had the disease, while those who did not have the gene were symptom-free. Further study of 100 normal people showed that none of them carried the defective gene. Neither did fourteen patients who had late onset Alzheimer's, a different form of the disorder that doesn't appear until the mid to late seventies.

Other studies verify Hardy's findings, and since this first study, Hardy has found two other genetic errors in families with Alzheimer's.

Even though hereditary factors do seem to play a role in the disease, the extent of the role is unclear. For example, studies done on identical twins, who share identical DNA, show that one twin may contract Alzheimer's while the other is spared.

Why this is so remains a mystery, but it is hypothesized that environmental factors such as lifestyle, diet, exposure to toxins, and level of mental activity all play a part. For this reason, attending to the suggestions in this book is of paramount importance. A change in lifestyle now may avert a change in mind and memory later.

There is some evidence that Alzheimer's may be caused by "slow viruses" that incubate in the brain for many years. Other researchers believe that people who have suffered a head injury, such as a fall or a car accident, or people who have been exposed to radiation, are at an increased risk for Alzheimer's.

For many years elevated amounts of aluminum have been reported in the brain tissue of Alzheimer's victims, but there is controversy over whether the high aluminum level in the brain is the cause of Alzheimer's disease, or a consequence of it.

Even so, most clinicians agree that avoiding aluminum is a good idea. In addition, a Canadian research team claims that they can reduce mental deterioration by giving a drug that eliminates aluminum from the body. For more information on aluminum, see Chapter 18, Neurotoxins and Memory.

RISK FACTORS FOR DEMENTIA

The risk for dementia doubles every 5 years between ages 65 and 85. Although aging is the largest risk factor for becoming demented, several other risk factors have been found to be significant

A family history of Dementia

The presence of dementia in a brother, sister, or a parent quadruples your risk of developing dementia. In those with two or more afflicted first degree relatives, the risk increases up to eight times. This is thought to be because of the higher probability of inheriting one or more of the genes which contribute to the development of the disease.

A family history of Down's syndrome

The presence of Down's syndrome in your family may increase your risk two to three times. The majority of people with Down's syndrome develop dementia, but dementia seems not to be caused by the genetic error that causes the syndrome, that is triplication of chromosome 21. It has been observed that family members *without* Down's syndrome who develop dementia do not have this genetic error.

A history of depression

It has been found that people who have suffered from depression more than ten years prior to the onset of dementia have approximately double the risk of developing the disease. The reasons for this are unclear, but reduced activity in the frontal and temporal lobes found in depression, along with imbalances in several neurotransmitters, may make the brain more vulnerable.

Estrogen deficiency

Estrogen deficiency in postmenopausal women has been implicated in a variety of studies as increasing the risk of Alzheimer's and other dementias. This has been found mostly in women who have had hysterectomies (including the ovaries). It is believed that the increased risk comes from estrogen's influence on nerve growth factor, which supports the neurons that contain acetylcholine.

Head trauma

Prolonged unconsciousness from head injuries, or multiple head injuries over time doubles the risk for dementia. This is thought to be caused by an increase of the protein beta-amyloid following head trauma. Beta amyloid is toxic to brain neurons and is found in the bundles of debris called *neuritic plaques* found in the brains of Alzheimer's victims.

Other possible risks for Dementia

Other factors that increase the risk for dementia include chronic alcohol consumption, a history of heart attack (especially in women), maternal age over 40, a family history of Parkinson's disease, and hypothyroidism—a deficiency in the activity of the thyroid gland.

Poor education

An uneducated person has about twice the risk of developing dementia by age 75 when compared to someone with at least an eighth grade education. This may be because education causes a strengthening of frequently used brain regions and enhances the connections between neurons. This strengthening of brain regions may also explain why some people with special talents, like playing music, playing cards, or singing may retain these skills after the onset of dementia. Recently several studies have shown a strong link between lower intelligence and dementing disease.

INTELLIGENCE AND ALZHEIMER'S

In a ground-breaking study, it was found that women who scored poorly in cognitive ability as young adults were found to be at higher risk for Alzheimer's disease in late life.

The study examined the cognitive function of nearly 100 nuns. Participants were members of the School Sisters of Notre Dame religious congregation. The study concentrated on those who joined the Milwaukee convent from 1931 through 1939 and who had written autobiographies at an average age of 22. They found that the complexity of the sisters' writings as young women was a good predictor of how they well they functioned mentally later in life.

In the study, it was found that 90% of the nuns with Alzheimer's disease had low linguistic ability in early life, compared with only 13% in those without the disease.

The researchers stated that why this happens is not clear. It may be that full development of the brain and cognitive abilities early in life, through education or other stimulation, may cause changes in the brain that protect people from Alzheimer's disease later in life.

Low linguistic ability in early life could actually be a very early symptom of changes in the brain that eventually lead to Alzheimer's disease.

Other factors could explain the link between early cognitive differences and disease in old age. It may be that inherited differences in cognitive ability, factors that may have nothing to do with the disease per se, may affect the way the Alzheimer's process unfolds in an individual.

Those with higher language ability early in life may be more resistant to later influences which lead to the disease while those with lower ability as young adults may be more at risk.

This study suggests that the process of Alzheimer's disease may begin much earlier in life than previously thought. These findings and other studies seem to indicate that brain cell deterioration may actually begin up to *thirty years* before any symptoms appear!

Research is now underway to detect these changes, in the hope that early intervention might prevent the devastating effects of the disease. New brain scan technology can pick up brain changes many years before symptoms appear.

DIAGNOSIS OF DEMENTIA

A complete medical assessment should be undertaken to help determine whether an individual has Alzheimer's. The fact that a person has the symptoms listed above does not automatically mean he or she is suffering from the disease. Symptoms can also be caused by other treatable conditions, such as depression, malnutrition, dehydration, over-medication, and other medical problems such as heart disease, kidney or lung problems.

The diagnosis of Alzheimer's is difficult, and is currently made only by ruling out other conditions. As of this writing, the only accurate method of diagnosing Alzheimer's is by a post-mortem examination of brain tissue. However, researchers have developed a genetic test for early onset Alzheimer's. Work is now in progress to develop a reliable MRI profile to diagnose the disease. Another test being researched detects beta-amyloid in spinal fluid, while still another method involves checking the ability of the eye to dilate.

People who appear to be showing any signs of dementia should have a thorough physical, psychological, and neurological screening. This should consist of a complete physical, including blood work, a cardiac work up, and possibly a brain scan. Brain scans can help rule out certain disorders, and may show that the problems are from normal aging rather than dementia.

A complete personal medical history, and family medical history should be taken. This should include a survey of all medications currently being taken, and a history of medications taken previously.

A competent neuropsychologist can be very helpful in screening for memory and cognitive deficits, and can often suggest effective therapies to alleviate many memory related symptoms.

TREATMENT

Currently, no approved medical treatment exists that can entirely reverse the progress of Alzheimer's. Secondary symptoms, such as depression, anxiety, sleeplessness and paranoia, may be lessened with appropriate drug therapy, though such treatments must be carefully monitored. The good news is that many of the substances described in this book show promise in slowing the progression of the disease.

Tetra-hydro-amino-acridine, or Tacrine, marketed under the brand name *Cognex*, is the only drug currently approved for the treatment of Alzheimer's. This drug has shown some promise in slowing and even reversing the progress of the disease, by slowing the breakdown of the neurotransmitter *acetylcholine*. Unfortunately, the magnitude of the changes in patients receiving Tacrine is small, even in responsive patients. In addition, although Tacrine has helped some patients, it has not been effective in all cases, and it has the potential to cause serious adverse effects.

The biggest problem with Tacrine is its potential to cause serious liver damage. More than 40% of patients given Tacrine showed increases in liver enzyme activity, and 51% of Tacrine-treated patients have adverse reactions related to treatment.

A team of Canadian and American researchers have found that a genetic test may help identify Alzheimer's patients that are most likely to benefit from Tacrine. The test shows which of three possible types of the ApoE gene that a patient carries. In their study, Tacrine was most effective in patients who didn't have the type called ApoE4. At least 35 % of Alzheimer's patients fall into this category. The finding is the first solid demonstration that a gene can predict response to a drug in the treatment of Alzheimer's

Because of the problems with Tacrine, other methods of prevention and treatment continue to be sought. So, even though Tacrine is at present the only drug approved for the treatment of Alzheimer's, other drugs are on the horizon.

As of this writing, several drugs are being developed that, like Tacrine, raise the level of acetylcholine through the inhibition of cholinesterase, the enzyme that breaks down acetylcholine in the body.

Pfizer/Eisai has a new medication called *donepezil* which will be on the market soon. Brand named *Aricept,* it has been approved by the FDA for experimental research on Alzheimer's sufferers. Other second-generation cholinesterase inhibitors include *metrifonate* (manufactured by Bayer), a drug with the experimental name *ENA 713* is being explored by Sandoz. A substance called *galanthamine*, and a sustained-release formula of *physostigmine* are also being developed. Two other drugs —*idazoxan*, and *guanfacine*, which is an antihypertensive medication, may be useful in combination with the new cholinergic drugs.

Linoprine is a drug that stimulates brain cells to release more acetylcholine. Another experimental drug, *HP749*, is said to amplify the neurotransmitter's signal.

Preliminary evidence suggests that many of these cholinesterase inhibitors may not only ameliorate symptoms, but they might alter the course of the disease itself. The new drugs may in fact reduce the production of beta amyloid, the protein component found in neuritic plaques, the bundles of debris found in brain cells of Alzheimer's patients.

Dr. Allen Roses headed the Duke University research team that first discovered an association between ApoE4 and Alzheimer's disease in 1993. Roses believes that ApoE testing could be used to assist in the diagnosis of patients with Alzheimer's symptoms, and to help determine the best treatment

The gene test is now being used by drug companies to see which subgroups of Alzheimer's patients will benefit from their experimental drugs. Among these new drugs is one called *S12024*, which seems to work best in patients who do carry the ApoE4 gene.

Nerve growth factor has shown promise in many animal studies, but has not yet been shown useful in humans. Another set of substances under study are those that stimulate *mitochondria,* the tiny energy factories within each brain cell. One promising substance is *acetyl-l-carnitine* (discussed in Chapter 23 of this book), while another potential treatment is a naturally occurring molecule called *substance P.*

Dr. Lon Schneider, the Pharmacology Program Director of the Alzheimer's Disease Research Center at the University of Southern California School of Medicine believes that the low levels of acetylcholine found in Alzheimer's sufferers may also respond to drugs that target other brain receptors called *muscarinic* and *nicotinic* receptors. Schneider believes that using several drugs at once that affect these various receptors could be more effective against symptoms than any single medication.

INFORMATION

More information about Alzheimer's Disease and other dementias can be obtained from the Alzheimer's Association, 919 N. Michigan Avenue, Chicago, IL 60611-1676. Their phone number is (800) 272-3900.

The Alzheimer's Disease Education and Referral Center is a clearinghouse of information which is supported by the National Institute of Aging. This organization also has information about vascular dementia. Their address is PO Box 8250, Silver Spring, MD 20907-8250.

MEMORY PROBLEMS QUESTIONNAIRE

I FORGET

1 The name of a movie star I see on television

2 The name of an old friend

3 The name of someone I am introducing

4 The name of someone to whom I was just introduced

5 The name of an object I am talking about

6 The name of one of my children

7 The title of a book I recently read

8 The title of a movie I recently saw

9 To take my vitamins

10 Whether I have taken my medication

11 Why I just walked into a room

12 To buy items at a store that I went there to get

13 To bring important material to a meeting or event

14 To defrost food for a meal

15 To keep commitments or promises

16 To return a phone call

17 To keep appointments

18 Where I parked my car

19 To pay bills on time

20 To do important tasks and chores

21 What time it is

22 Where I put an important object

23 To turn off my headlights

24 What I was about to say to someone

25 Where I was born

26 If I have already told someone a story

27 The details of a story I am telling

28 What day of the week it is

29 What month it is

30 Where I am

31 The plot of a book or movie I have read or seen

32 Whether I have eaten

33 A close friend's or relative's birthday

34 Instructions I have just been given

35 A good friend's telephone number

36 To whom I lent something

37 What I have just read

IMPORTANT MEMORY PROBLEMS

2, 5, 6, 17, 25, 26, 29, 30, 32, 35

If you answered yes to these questions, you should seek professional help.

CHAPTER SIX

HOW TO STUDY

Study is the deliberate effort to memorize or learn new information. The goal of study is to be able to recognize, recall, and reproduce what you have learned.

WHY STUDY?

Unfortunately the vast majority of us stop studying the minute we finish school. But hundreds of research papers on memory point to the fact that *studying and learning new skills is one of the most powerful ways to maintain a healthy memory.*

For this reason, I highly recommend that you make a commitment to learn something new. Pick something you know very little about, and make the decision to master it. Take a class, read a book, attend a seminar—do what ever you like the most—but learn something new.

Don't tell me that you're too old to go to school. When I was in graduate school, a lady in my class got her doctorate at 73 and set up a private practice. You're never too old to learn something.

Why is this so important? Researchers like Marian Diamond have shown clearly that the more the mind is challenged to learn new things, the better that memory functions. Studies show that learning new things actually increases the number of connections between brain cells, and causes the cells to remain healthy and active. Clearly, studying is one of the most impor- tant and effective ways to maintain a powerful memory.

Even though this is true, it's a sad fact that most of us hate to study. Why is this so?

It isn't that we hate to learn—learning is fun—it's study- ing that we hate. We hate feeling stupid. We hate the frustration that comes when we can't understand something. We hate hav- ing to spend hours on something that we aren't interested in and don't care about.

Most people associate studying with school, homework, and taking tests. For these reasons, study seems like drudgery. Everyone remembers walking away from a study session feeling that they hadn't learned anything.

People dislike studying because studying:

> *is seen as punishment*
> *makes people feel stupid*
> *makes people feel frustrated*
> *provokes the feeling of failure*
> *was never learned properly*
> *destroys self esteem*

But take heart. If you follow the suggestions in this section, your ability to study will improve. Consider each one of these suggestions, as they are all proven techniques for improving your study habits. Once you have become an expert at studying, you will enjoy it more. Eventually you will feel that studying can actually be fun!

Studying is good because:

> *It is stimulating to learn new information.*
> *You will gain a sense of accomplishment as you begin to master a new subject.*
> *You will have the feeling that you are doing something good for yourself*
> *A class can be a social event where you meet new people.*
> *This is an opportunity to challenge yourself again and again.*
> *The class will give you something to share with your friends and loved ones.*
> *You will keep our memory sharp*

Your immediate goal is to turn new study skills into habits. Once you have done this, you'll automatically do the things necessary for studying effectively. Once this happens, your mind will thank you.

STRUCTURE YOUR TIME

The first and most important factor in learning something is the structuring of time. Most of us take on new projects thinking we can do a great deal more than we actually can do. This is because we always have more enthusiasm when we begin a project then after we're halfway through it. So don't overload yourself; take on a project you can handle.

Overloading the day ruins the enjoyment of it. Obviously, if you have more things to do than you have hours to do them in, you won't get all of your work done. But in addition to not completing your work, you rush through the work you do attempt, feeling distracted and anxious.

When you overload your day, you end up doing poorly in everything. Instead of concentrating on the things you are doing, you worry about what you still need to do, and feel guilty about what you didn't do. And at the end of the day, you can't remember anything that you did. If you've ever reached the bottom of a page only to realize you have no idea what you just read, you know how preoccupation destroys concentration

It is important to get a realistic picture of how long it takes to accomplish certain tasks. Experience with hundreds of people has taught me that most of us are very bad at estimating how long things take.

The best way find out how long a task actually takes is to do the task and time yourself. For example, find out how long it takes you to read a page in a book, or find out how long it takes you do the laundry.

Don't fret if it takes you longer to do something than it takes someone else. No matter how much time it takes you, if you organize your time well, and don't take on more work than you can handle, you'll to have enough time to finish everything.

Make a structured daily schedule of activities. This schedule should include study time and your activity schedule for each day.

Don't forget to schedule in fun along with daily and weekly obligations. No one looks forward to a day that contains only work.

People tell me that they object to scheduling their entire day. They claim that schedules are too restricting. They want to be able to be free to do *what* they want to do *when* they feel like it.

This sounds good, but it just isn't true.

First of all, it is *you* who are making this schedule, so you actually do decide what you will do and when. Second, you already know that you put off or forget to do things that you don't like to do. So, if you wait until you feel like doing it, it never gets done.

Third, you will find that after you begin to schedule your time, you will actually feel more free to do the things you want to do. It is much easier to enjoy leisure time when you don't have that guilty feeling in the back of your mind that your obligations haven't been met.

Fourth, *scheduling improves self-esteem, reduces stress, is an effective antidepressant, and greatly improves memory.*

Even if you don't work, schedules are important. As you check off the things you do each day, you get a feeling of accomplishment and satisfaction. You feel productive. This is very different from the feeling of rushing through a day, forgetting important things, going to bed each night wondering where the time went, and feeling like the day was wasted.

Planning the day has long term effects too. Keeping a schedule allows you to look back over the weeks and months to remind yourself of all the things you have accomplished. This helps you deal with that "where did the time go?" feeling.

Most importantly, schedules reduce anxiety and improve the ability to concentrate, learn, and remember.

Although keeping a schedule may be a bother at first, after a few weeks of scheduling, planning the day will become a natural thing, and you won't think of it as a chore.

SCHOOL AND STUDY

Taking a class is one of the most effective ways to keep your memory sharp. The stimulation of new information, new skills, and new people keeps the mind alert.

If you decide to take a class or seminar, go to all of the sessions. Even if you don't enjoy a certain session, resist the temptation to skip it, and show up every time. Remind yourself of the reason you took the class in the first place—to improve your memory. Don't worry about how well you do in the class. Remember that your goal is to learn something, not to be the smartest person in the room.

PREPARE A STUDY ENVIRONMENT

Where and when you study is just as important as how you study. Studying should be done in a quiet, private place where there are no distractions or interruptions. If you study at home, find a place away from other family members and other distractions, such as the TV or radio.

Tell friends, neighbors and relatives that you have set aside a certain time to study, and you don't wish to be disturbed. This is sometimes not enough, however, and people may still drop over or call you during your study time. Make a firm commitment not to answer the door or telephone during your study time. After everyone realizes that you are serious about not being disturbed, they will quit interrupting you, and your time will be your own.

I strongly recommend that you do not have a TV or radio playing when you are studying. Although you may be used to this and enjoy it, it adds nothing to the ability to study, and it can, and does distract you from time to time, and it will break your concentration.

If you have taught yourself to study or read with the radio on, it may be a tough habit to break. However, after a few weeks of practice, you will get used to the silence, and have better results in learning and retention.

Research on aging and memory shows that the older we get, the more difficult it becomes to filter out distractions, so minimize them.

STUDY DO'S AND DON'TS

- Do structure your time, using a realistic assessment of how much you can accomplish.
- Don't miss classes.
- Do create a quiet place for study where you will not be disturbed.
- Do sit at an uncluttered desk or table as you study.
- Do try to study at the same place at the same time each day.
- Don't skip meals.
- Do study at the times of the day when you naturally have more energy.
- Don't skimp on sleep.

CREATE A STUDY SPACE

Study at a desk or table, and sit in a chair. Don't study standing up, lying down, or sprawled out on a bed. Although these positions may be appealing to you, you will tire faster than you will sitting in a chair at a study table, and you'll get less done. Have you ever fallen asleep while reading? Sitting up makes this less likely.

Make sure that your study table or desk is large enough to hold all the materials that you need. See that your table or desk does not face an open window or door, both of which can be a source of distraction. Have all of your materials and study tools such as pens, pencils, erasers and rulers, available to you before you begin studying. This eliminates interruptions in your work because you are looking around for the item you need.

Clear the desk of everything that isn't needed for the subject you are studying. Clutter makes it hard to concentrate, and if you put other unrelated material on your desk, it will be a constant reminder of what you have not yet finished.

Make sure that the lighting is adequate, and that the room temperature is comfortable. You will have less ability to concentrate in a room that is too cold, or too warm.

GO TO THE LIBRARY

If you don't have a good study space in your home, consider studying in you nearest library. Surveys show that people learn more effectively when they study in libraries.

There are several reasons why a library is a good place to study:

• **Studying in a library gets you out of your house.** It's a way to break the habit of isolation and boredom, as well as getting you away from all the distractions you find at home, such as television, the refrigerator, or a friendly looking couch.

• Because you are away from home, **you are less likely to be interrupted.** People rarely drop by the library just to visit you.

• A library is a place of learning, and **just walking into a library puts you in the right frame of mind to learn something.** Those who study in libraries find that they get more done in less time for these reasons.

DEVELOP A "STUDY SET"

Study the same subject in the same place, at the same time of day if possible. Doing this will allow you to develop what psychologists call a *response set*, that will help put you in the right frame of mind to study. Objects in your environment, and feelings that you experience at a certain time of day can act as cues to tell you that it is time to study. This will happen in the same way that turning on the television prompts some people to think that it is time to eat. Once you do develop this study habit, sitting down at your desk at three o'clock will automatically put you in the mood to learn.

FOOD AND STUDY

What and when you eat can have an effect on your ability to study. It is not a good idea to study right after you have eaten a heavy meal, as this tends to make you feel tired and sluggish, and you won't pay attention to what you are studying. On the other hand, it is not a good idea to skip meals in order to try to get more done.

Skipping meals can result in low blood sugar. Low blood sugar makes it harder to concentrate, makes you easily irritated and frustrated, and will cause you to walk away from your study session with the feeling that the work is too much to deal with.

When the negative feelings caused by low blood sugar happen at the same time that you are studying, you'll associate those feelings with what you are studying, and you'll avoid that subject in the future, without ever really knowing why you don't like it.

Meals high in carbohydrate can make you drowsy, while a high protein meal can sharpen your mind. Its also been shown that eating immediately *after* you study can improve memory storage. Researchers have found that eating causes the release of the hormone *cholecsytokynin*, which improves memory.

As mentioned earlier in this book, fragrances become associated with information and can be used as a study aid. Smelling citrus, mint, or chocolate that you have placed in your pocket while you study can help you recall information when you use the same scent during a test.

DRUGS AND STUDY

During an intense study period, some people smoke cigarettes and drink a lot of coffee. Both of these drugs affect your memory and your ability to study. When you study under the influence of drugs such as nicotine, caffeine, or other stimulants, you create a situation that is called *state dependence.*

State dependence is the phenomenon of not being able to recall material that you learned while in a certain state of mind until you are in that state again. If you're using stimulants while studying, you will have trouble remembering what you studied unless you use the same stimulants again. This makes you dependant on a drug to be able to recall what you have learned, which is a less than desirable situation. For this reason, you should try to avoid studying while under the influence of any drug. (More information on caffeine appears in Chapter 17 and on smoking in chapter 18.)

BIOLOGICAL CLOCKS

Whenever it's possible, arrange your study time to fit your energy cycle. All of us have a natural daily energy cycle. For most of us, this cycle has two peaks, one in the morning, and one in the evening. There is usually a slump between the peaks, which occurs in mid-afternoon, often about two o'clock. If you are a morning person, the best time to study is before noon, when you are at your energy peak. If you are a night person, the best time to study is in the evening, usually somewhere between three in the afternoon and ten at night.

For most of us, the time period from about noon to three is our *midday slump*. During this time of day the ability to concentrate is low. Studying during midday slump will result in poorly learned material, or an unintended nap! Scheduling your study time to match your energy peaks will increase your ability to concentrate, and increase your tolerance for frustration.

SLEEP AND STUDY

The amount of sleep that you get can also affect your ability to absorb and retain new information. Lack of sleep makes for inefficient study and poor memory. Many people get into the habit of studying late at night, when things are quiet, and others are sleeping.

Aside from the fact that your energy and tolerance for frustration are lower at night, if you study late, and have to attend a class early in the morning, you won't get enough sleep.

Lack of sleep results in chronic fatigue, and it lowers your resistance to illness. It also can result in extreme nervousness and irritability and interferes with the ability to concentrate.

Each of us has a minimum number of hours required for proper rest. While a few people can get by on as little as six or seven hours of sleep a night, others need as much as ten hours of sleep each night in order to feel rested. Don't feel guilty or lazy if you require more sleep than some of your friends. The amount of sleep that you need is set biologically, and it is a myth that we all need eight hours sleep. Robbing your body of as little as a half hour's sleep can impair concentration.

If you require an alarm clock to wake you up each morning, you may in fact not be getting enough sleep. If you are not getting enough rest, and are studying when you are tired and irritable, you may begin to associate the subject that you are studying with the irritability. Later you may find yourself avoiding that subject, thinking that it is the cause of the irritation. In reality you are irritated merely because you are tired.

THE STUDY PROCESS

You will become a better student if you consider the following crucial factors:

Intend to remember

When you want to record something in your memory that you don't find interesting, you must do so with conscious, deliberate intent. To do this, prepare yourself for memorizing, by telling yourself that you are going to remember. If possible, sit quietly for a few moments before you start, and relax. Take a few deep breaths, clear your mind, and tell yourself that you are about to memorize something, and that you are going to remember it perfectly. While this might seem silly, think of what you normally do. Many people prepare for memorizing by saying things like, "Boy, this stuff is boring. I'll never remember it!" That sounds even sillier. Since you already talk to yourself, learn to do so in a positive manner.

Write it down

Writing something down *triples* the odds that you will remember it. Writing involves visual, motor, and informational memory, and forces you to pay attention to what you want to learn. People who take notes learn significantly faster than those who don't.

Get organized

How you structure your study session affects how much you accomplish during that session. Once you have a place and a time in which to study, make a study plan. Know in advance what it is you intend to accomplish during your study session, and write these things down.

If you are planning to study more than one subject, *study the most difficult subject first.* In this way your energy level and tolerance for frustration will be higher when you are working on difficult material. If you save the most difficult subject for last, you'll be tired before you even start, and the work will seem more difficult than it actually is. When this happens, you'll give up too easily, and avoid the subject completely.

If you have scheduled your time properly, the fact that a difficult subject takes more time will not prevent you from completing your other work.

Keep focused

When interest is low, the human attention span is quite short. The brain has an automatic mechanism which diverts attention from unimportant information. (See the section in Chapter 3 on the *orienting response*). The way to force yourself to pay attention is to read the material out loud, and write down what you want to remember. Doing this forces you to pay attention.

Educators have discovered that the most effective way to learn something is by using the *spaced-practice method.* Spend a short time reading the material, take a break, and look at it again. Do this many times throughout the day.

During your allotted study time, break up your study sessions into short periods of time—about twelve to fifteen minutes each. This is the best time span for maximum concentration.

When you find your attention repeatedly wandering, take a break and try again later. Separate different subjects with breaks also. This will allow you to mentally prepare yourself for the next subject.

Set reasonable goals

Set a goal for each short study period. For each fifteen or twenty minute period, know exactly what you plan to learn. For example, tell yourself that in the next hour you will have memorized and learned how to use five French verbs. Don't expect to memorize an entire book at one sitting. You will set yourself up for failure. At the end of that study period, test yourself to see that you've accomplished your goal. If you find that you are not reaching your goals, set them lower.

Make sure it means something

It's more likely that you will remember a sentence spoken in English than one spoken in Russian. The things we remember easily are things that we already understand.

For example, if you are a baseball fan, you can watch a game on television and later tell your friends about it in vivid detail. You can do this because you already have an understanding of the rules of the game. On the other hand, you might attend a lecture on theoretical physics and walk away not remembering a thing.

Because memory works on the principle of association, it is important that you understand something about the material before you can memorize it. This enables you to associate the material with something you already know.

For this reason, it's important that you develop a broad background on the subject that you need to assimilate. This means that you must spend some time learning the basics about that subject before you attempt to memorize the new information. One of my clients was a secretary in a company that sold hydraulic equipment. One of her duties was to read reports that came to the office, and give her boss a verbal summary of what she had read. She was having a terrible time doing this because she could not remember the technical terms in the reports.

Upon my suggestion, she bought an introductory text-book on hydraulics, and read it every night after work. As she began to understand the theory of hydraulics, she was able to remember the terminology, because now she understood what the words meant.

Become an expert in the area that you want to master, and you will memorize new material easily. Take pride in your expertise, and it will motivate you to remember.

Repeat and rehearse

You know that if you see or hear something enough, you remember it whether you want to or not. Just think of all the TV and radio commercials you've learned without any conscious effort. Use the principle of *over-learning*. Tape the information and play it to yourself twenty times a day. Put it on flash cards and tape them up everywhere.

Test yourself

Using self tests is an excellent way to discover how much you have learned. It also allows you to eliminate studying material you already know. Flash cards are a good system of self-testing. But the best way to verify that you have learned something is to explain it to someone else. If you can put what you have learned in your own words, you know that it has been stored in your long term memory.

CHAPTER SEVEN

HOW TO STOP LOSING AND FORGETTING THINGS

How many hours of your life have you wasted looking for lost sunglasses, car keys, your shoes, or your wallet or purse? Time management experts say that the average person spends about four weeks per year looking for misplaced objects!

Looking for lost objects is not only time wasting, it's also frustrating. So why do you find yourself doing this again and again?

You lose things for three reasons.

First, you have never made a commitment to fix the problem. In fact, you only become aware of the problem when it's happening. What you need to do is make a commitment right now to stop losing things.

Second, without being aware of it, you've developed habits that help you lose things. For example, you put your keys down wherever you feel like putting them. You set your sunglasses down anywhere when you take them off. You put important papers on any available flat space.

Third, you put things down without paying attention to what you are doing. You remember only what you consciously pay attention to, so it's not surprising that you can't remember what you've done. For this reason, many inanimate objects seem to roam aimlessly around the house.

You will stop losing things when you foster habits in yourself that help you find them.

Here are some solutions:

- First and most importantly, **make a list of the things that you keep losing.** Next to each item on the list, write down what you intend to do to stop losing it. Write down the place where you will store each item. Keep this list posted where you can see it so that it becomes a reminder of where things are.

- **Establish a specific place for each item, and to always put things in their place.** Doing this involves breaking old, unconscious habits. To break these habits, put signs up around the house to remind you to put things in their proper place. For example, make a sign that says "The bills go here."

- **Put labels on cabinets and drawers that tell you what is to be stored in them.** Label storage boxes and canisters also, so you know what they contain.

- **Use clear plastic storage boxes** for small items like screws and buttons, and label them also.

- **Put labels with your name address and phone number on objects that you often take out of the** house, such as umbrellas and glasses. This increases the odds that you will get them back if you do forget them.

- When you are out of your house, *carry everything in one bag* if possible, and attach the bag to your clothing so that you can't lose it.

- When you sit down in a restaurant, **put the bag on the table** so it is in plain sight. This makes it hard to forget it. If you must carry several items with you, know how many items you left with, make a checklist of them before you leave the house, and look at the list each time you leave a location.

- Teach yourself to look at what you are doing, and **say out loud exactly where you are putting something.** When you put your keys on the coffee table, say out loud, "I'm putting my keys on the coffee table." Saying out loud what you are doing insures that you are paying attention to your actions. While you might laugh at this idea, when you begin to use it, you won't lose anything again. Practice recalling where you put things just to make sure you remember.

- Whenever possible, **buy several of what you often lose.** This works well for items like pens, scissors, tape, glue, batteries, and other utility items. Put some of the items in several places around your house and office. It will save you hours of frustration. For example, if you have a pair of scissors in every room in your house, you won't have to wander from room to room looking for them.

- Protect yourself from family thievery by **buying a set of household items for each family member.** Make each member responsible for their own scissors, pencils, and glue.

- When you are parking your car in a large parking structure, **write down where the car is parked on the parking ticket, and put the ticket in your pocket.** Look around the area and make a mental note of any landmarks that you can associate with the car's location.

- Finally, **don't loan anyone anything you value without getting a written statement from them that they have taken it.** If you don't do this, you'll never see it again, and you won't know who to ask.

- If you have lost something, **go back in time to the last time you remember seeing it.** Retrace your steps until you happen upon it. If this doesn't work, imagine where you would put the item if you had it, and look there. Start with the obvious places, and work towards the less likely spots.

- If you have to do this with an item more than once, **add it to your list of frequently lost items.**

Have you ever had someone tell you, "It's right under your nose?" Psychologist Yvette Tenny researched people's experiences searching for lost objects. She discovered that many times the object was in fact in the very place a person had looked. They had simply failed to recognize it. The older a person was, the more likely this was to occur. She felt that this experience was caused by a decrease in perceptual ability that occurs with age. Her findings suggest that the next time you lose something, you might try looking in each spot twice.

Exercise: Hide & Seek

Here's an exercise to test your ability to remember where you put things.

Put about ten items away one evening.

Before you go to bed, write down where you stowed these objects away.

The next day, attempt to recover all of the items without looking at the list.

This exercise will help you get into the habit of making mental notes about where you put things.

HOW TO STOP FORGETTING THINGS

Now that you are armed with ideas that will help you stop losing things, here are some additional tips that will help you kick the habit of forgetting:

- **When a thought occurs to you that you should do something, do it immediately**. If you do not, you will forget. If you cannot do it immediately, write it down in an appointment book, so that you will see it later that day. When this Idea occurred to me, I immediately wrote it down.

- **Use a daily medication and nutritional supplement box** to insure you have taken the proper pills each day. Fill the box at the end of each week.

- **Use an alarm clock to remind you to do important things.** Set several alarms around the house as reminders for important events. For example, if you need to call someone at seven, set the alarm for that time. If needed, put a note next to the alarm so that when you shut it off, you will remember why you set it.

- **Use an appointment book whether you work or not.** The book adds structure to your day and reminds you what you need to do, and what you have done.

- **Record your thoughts, ideas, and things to do on tape.** Establish a time of day to play the tape back and write the material down in your daily planning book.

- **When writing notes to yourself, compose them as if you were writing them to someone else.** This will allow you to understand them when you read them later. For example, instead of writing "Call Dick at 7:30," write, "You talked to Dick Smith today about the computer he wants to sell. Call him at 7:30 on Tuesday, April 20, and tell him when you will pick it up."

- **Attach your car keys to Items you need to take with you when you leave the house.** This way you cannot leave without them.

- **When you are cooking, do not answer the door or telephone, or go into another room to watch tele-**

vision. Stay at the stove and you won't burn things (including your house!).

• **Whenever you are cooking something that must be timed, use a timer with an alarm.** Don't rely on remembering to look at the clock—you are asking for trouble, and you will spoil your meal.

With a little added effort you can greatly reduce the amount of things you lose and forget. You'll feel less frustrated as a result. And think of all the time you will save yourself.

REMEMBERING NAMES

Because forgetting names is the most common memory problem, I'd like to review some tips for correcting it. The trick is to make a special effort to remember them.

Before you go to any social gathering, review the names of the people you expect to see. If you can't bring the names to mind, ask someone else for the information. You might even call your host and get a guest list. Rehearse the names in your mind several times. Before you arrive at the event, form memory links by linking things you know about the individual with their name.

Gather personal information about new people you meet, and form a link between the data and the name. For example, Barry is a golfer, so think of him burying his clubs after a bad game. When possible, collect business cards from each person you meet. Write information about the person on the back of the card to remind you who they are.

Keep a small "name bank" book with the names, descriptions, and personal information about people you will see again. Make a habit of reviewing the book frequently.

Everyone has said at some time, "I can never remember his name." If you repeatedly forget a certain person's name, resolve to fix the problem. Take a few moments to visualize the person. Rehearse the name several times. Think of someone else with the same name and say to yourself something like, "His name is Jerry, just like Jerry Clark next door."

CHAPTER EIGHT

FACTORS FOR MAXIMIZING MEMORY

Whenever you're having difficulty remembering anything, ask yourself the following questions.

AM I PAYING ATTENTION?

Make a conscious effort to focus on the material you wish to memorize. One way to do this is to say out loud whatever you wish to remember. Saying things out loud forces you to pay attention.

AM I INTERESTED?

Interest is the most important deciding factor whether you will remember something. The more interested you are in something the easier it is to remember. You can increase your interest in something simply by learning more about it. For example, sports fans remember a remarkable amount of information about sports because the are emotionally invested in it. Because they already know a lot about the field, new information comes easy.

IS IT AROUSING?

The things that we are interested in stir our emotions. This is why you are able to remember the plot of a good movie more easily than a chapter in your history book. If you absolutely can't get aroused about the material, get aroused by challenging your self to remember it. Dare yourself to remember.

IS IT IMPORTANT?

Most of us have no trouble remembering to pick up our paychecks. We remember things that are important to us. You can increase the importance of something if you focus on the benefits of remembering it. In other words, what's the payoff?

AM I MOTIVATED TO REMEMBER?

If you know that you will benefit by remembering something, you are more motivated to remember it. For example, if someone told you that they would pay you $5,000 for remembering their name the next time you saw them, you would most likely make a special effort to remember it.

If you can't clearly see the payoff for remembering something, use the information as an opportunity to practice the memory techniques you learned in this book. Another way to get motivated about remembering something is to think of the consequences of remembering or forgetting it.

For example, if you need to get a few things from the store after work, think of the benefits of remembering to do it. If you do remember, you will save yourself an extra trip. Now think of the consequences of not remembering. If you forget, you must go back to the store, and besides wasting time, you might make someone angry. In other words, remembering will make things easier on you.

WHAT'S MY ATTITUDE?

A negative attitude about a piece of information lowers your chances of remembering. A negative attitude can cause you to ignore something that might be important to remember. You may even actively avoid the subject you need to remember. Have you ever found yourself saying, "I keep forgetting to do such and such," or, "No matter how much I study this, I just can't remember it!" This kind of negative programming is like a self-fulfilling prophesy. If you tell yourself that you can't remember something, you probably won't.

IS IT WEIRD OR DIFFERENT?

You remember things that are unusual or out of the ordinary. For example, if you meet ten people a day, you might have trouble remembering their names, but if one of them was seven feet tall with green hair, you will remember her because she was different.

You can make an ordinary thing novel by learning it a new way. For example, one of my students was studying accounting. She made it interesting by cutting her textbook into pieces, and sticking the pieces up all over her house.

DID I WRITE IT DOWN?

You will triple that odds of remembering something simply by writing it down. Writing involves focused attention, motor

FACTORS AFFECTING MEMORY

EXTERNAL FACTORS	INTERNAL FACTORS
The amount of interfering stimuli	Interest in the event
The novelty of the event	Deliberate Intent to remember
The emotional impact	Paying Attention
The complexity of the event	Your personal level of background knowledge
The structure of the event (is it logical or chaotic?)	Level of arousal
The number of times the event occurs	Your internal model for organizing the data
	Your mood

memory, and visual memory, three things that insure memory storage.

DID I REPEAT IT?

Advertisers know that repeated messages are remembered. Use this fact to insure memory storage. Repeat the desired material several times during the day, and it will record itself in long term memory.

AM I USING A SYSTEM?

Research studies show that the older one gets, the less likely it is that they use a memory system. Learning and using memory systems can double your memory in just a few days. For information on memory systems, turn the pages to the next chapter.

CHAPTER NINE

MEMORY SYSTEMS

Almost every survey of memory problems shows one major difference between people over forty and the younger population—the majority of people over forty do not use memory systems. In fact, the majority of adults in the over-forty group have never been taught these systems, and have little interest in learning them.

This is unfortunate, because when researchers looked at the differences between older people with memory problems and those who had superior memories, they again found one glaring difference—those with good memories used memory systems.

Even though most adults have never heard of these systems, they are far from new. In fact, most memory systems date back at least to the era of ancient Greece.

Before paper and the printing press were invented, all important information had to be memorized. Early Greek and Roman teachers and orators were able to memorize large amounts of information by using some simple memory techniques. Most of these techniques are still in use today.

Although there are many different kinds of memory systems all take advantage of the basic properties of memory—*association and visualization.*

ASSOCIATION

When you are exposed to a new piece of information, your mind automatically executes a search for associations. You make associations through several principles: similarity, contrast, contiguity, continuity, and synesthesia .

The quality of *similarity* insures that our minds automatically link any bits of information that share characteristics. These similarities may be obvious, as linking words that rhyme, or may be as subtle as your Uncle Henry's alleged resemblance to Victor Mature.

The quality of *contrast* causes us to link things with their perceived opposites. The word "hot" instantly brings to mind "cold."

The quality of association by *contiguity* occurs when two or more things happen together in time and place. Even though they have no intrinsic similarity, because they happened together, they become associated. Advertisers have used this quality of the mind for years—the shiny new car will get us the pretty girl. And even though we say we know better, our mind makes the link.

Associations based on *continuity* are similar to contiguous associations. With continuity things become linked because of their order and sequence. Obvious examples of this are the alphabet and the number system.

We know the sequence of our alphabet and number system not because of any intrinsic need for the letters to be in a certain order—we just learned them that way. Very few people can recite the alphabet backwards.

Our language contains specific structures also. A sentence is comprehensible not only because we understand the words, but because we anticipate its structure. A string of words out of sequence is much more difficult to remember than a sentence.

Less obvious are things like story-telling. In our culture, we learn to tell stories in a specific way, with a clear beginning, middle, and end. Stories in which one element is missing, or where the parts are out of sequence, are much harder to comprehend and remember. By the time we are four years old, we have learned how to structure a story properly.

Synesthetic associations are those that cross over sensory boundaries. People who have a highly developed synesthetic sense can literally see noises, taste colors, and feel music.

These types of associations make no intrinsic sense, but are very real and often quite vivid. For example, a woman I was working with told me, "My boyfriend reminds me of mashed potatoes." She could not tell me why, but every time she thought of him, mashed potatoes came to mind. And ever since I was a kid, Franky Avalon has reminded me of Vienna sausage.

Since memory already makes these kinds of associations unconsciously and automatically, it makes sense to deliberately and consciously start using this ability to help memory.

Here's some examples of how association helps memory: Read the following number:

1 7 7 6 1 9 8 4 2 0 0 11 0 5

Now close your eyes and repeat the number. You probably could not do this. One of the reasons for this is that 15 digits is too much for you to store in your short-term memory.

One way to remember the number is to cut it into pieces. This cutting of information into more digestible segments is called *chunking*.

Scan the number and associate it with things that you already know. Some of my students notice that the first twelve digits contain dates which are the titles of three movies:

1776   1984   2001

That's a great way to remember these numbers. Now for the last three digits, 105, visualize yourself wearing a pair of Levi's 501's backwards.

To remember the whole number, think of yourself seeing the movies, 1776, 1984 and 2001 while wearing your Levi's 501's backwards (for 105).

Let's do it another way, by cutting the number into five pieces. Five is less than seven, the maximum number you can process with you short term memory.

Here are the chunks:

177   619   842   001   105

Now let's make a specific association with each chunk. Look at the first three digits, 177. Here's an association one of my students gave me. He said that's what he drank every day after work: one seven and seven.

The second three numbers, 619, is the area code for San Diego. If you live in California, this association is immediate.

The third three numbers, 842, can be remembered as "ate for two." The fourth three digits are 001, which is James Bond's grandfather. The fifth three digits, 105, is a pair of blue jeans backwards (again think of Levi's 501's).

Now let's take this second group of associations and link them together. To do this, we'll use the second automatic property of memory, visualization.

VISUALIZATION

Visualizing is the ability to form pictures in your mind. Some of you know that you are good visualizers, and some of you believe that you are poor at visualizing, or that you can't visualize at all.

For reasons not yet completely understood, as people age, they use their visualization skills less. This loss of visual imagery is a major contributor to age associated memory impairment.

Even so, everyone has this ability, and everyone can improve it with practice. In order to demonstrate that this is true, I'm going to ask you to participate in a little experiment.

Close your eyes, and count the number of windows in your house. Take a moment to mentally travel from room to room, and tally the number of windows that you see.

How many windows did you count? In order for you to do this exercise, you had to form a mental picture. This means that you *are* able to visualize, and it also means that you will be able to use the memory systems that I am about to describe.

THE LINK SYSTEM

The *link system* of memorization uses visualization and association to link together unrelated items on a list. Telling a story is more interesting than memorizing a list, and enhances your ability to memorize any list of words. The link system uses visual links to tie together unrelated items. Here's how it works.

Let's go back now to that 15 digit number. In your imagination, see a man at a bar drinking one seven and seven. He picks up the phone on the bar to call San Diego. After he ate for two (see him sitting with a huge pile of food in front of him), he becomes upset when he sees James Bond's grandfather thrown out of the bar for wearing his Levi's backwards.

You now have formed a visual memory of the number. Once these pictures are in place, this number will stay in your memory forever.

Now, take a moment to read the following list of words:

1. FISH	6. HOUSE
2. BED	7. FORK
3. TABLE	8. WINDOW
4. BOTTLE	9. KNEE
5. PAPER	10. FLY

These words are not related to one another in any logical way. They do not tell a story, and would be difficult to remember without a system. But by using the link system, the words will become indelibly associated forever. As you read each item do the following:

1. FISH. See a six foot tall albacore tuna walking through his house.

2. BED. The fish walks into his bedroom, and plops down on his California king size water bed.

3. TABLE. His wife comes in carrying his breakfast on a small table, and places it on his bed.

4. BOTTLE. On the table is a small brown wine bottle.

5. PAPER. Out of the neck of the bottle sticks a rolled up sheet of paper.

6. HOUSE. Imagine taking the paper out of the bottle and flattening it out. On the paper is a picture of Mr. and Mrs. Fish's house.

7. FORK. You immediately notice that there is a 27 foot fork sticking out of the top of the house.

8. WINDOW. When you look closely at this giant fork, you notice that cut into the end of the handle is a window.

9. KNEE. Sticking through the window is a large human knee.

10. FLY. On the kneecap is a fly.

Once you have formed these associative and visual links in your mind, you have memorized the list. You can now recite the list forwards and backwards. Try it.

THE LOCUS SYSTEM

The *locus system* involves associating the things that you wish to remember with familiar landmarks in your environment. For demonstration purposes, let's memorize a short shopping list. It consists of ten items. Without a memory system, it is difficult for you to remember ten items, because your short term memory can only hold seven or eight items.

See how many of the items on the shopping list you can remember without writing them down.

broccoli	potato chips
lettuce	tomatoes
mayonnaise	hamburger
hot dogs	a copy of the *Enquirer*
peanut butter	a jar of mustard

A moment ago you counted the windows in your house. Now, associate each item on the list with a window in your house. Get a clear picture of the item in the window. Once this picture has been solidified, a mental walk through the house will remind you of the items. (If you live in a place with doesn't have enough windows, you can use items of furniture.)

READING TO REMEMBER

How many times have you found yourself at the bottom of a page, with absolutely no memory of what you have just read? Although we have all done this when reading for pleasure, it is even more common when reading a textbook. People hate to read textbooks because many of them are boring and complicated. You will save time and increase your comprehension of your reading material if you approach reading with a plan.

Most people object to plans, and prefer to read a chapter as they would a novel. They unrealistically hope that one reading will allow them to absorb all the information. Others use a highlighter to mark the things they feel are important. Most do this with the intent to read the chapter again later. Of course, they rarely do.

Taking notes while you read eliminates these problem. Taking notes forces you to pay attention to what you are reading. And reading your notes is much easier than re-reading an entire chapter.

A chapter of text is pre-structured, but you can impose your own structure on the material. For example, history is the study and interpretation of the past. Important information in history consists of names, dates, deeds and events. Divide a piece of paper into four columns with the headings:

NAMES   DATES   DEEDS   EVENTS

Now skim through the chapter and list all material that belongs under each of these headings. In this manner, with one reading, you've extracted all the important information from the chapter.

I also find it very useful to use a cassette recorder when I am reading to remember. Every time I come across a point I feel I should remember, I put it on tape. When I'm finished reading, I have an audio summary of what I want to know which I can play back in my car as many times as necessary.

THE KEY WORD SYSTEM

The *key word system* is used in memorizing reading material and speeches. It involves extracting key words from the text to act as hooks to recover the material. This is similar to making an outline. Doing this doubles the probability that you will remember the material. For example, take the paragraph topics of the chapter or the speech, and then connect them using the link system described earlier in this chapter. This simple tool can prevent you from losing your train of thought when giving a presentation.

THE PHONETIC CODE SYSTEM

The *phonetic code system* is one of the most widely used memory techniques. It involves assigning a number value to the consonant sounds in the English language. In this manner, long strings of numbers can be transformed into familiar words. This technique allows you to memorize long numbers almost instantly. See the chart for the letter codes on the next page.

Through the use of this system, any number can be converted into a few words that result in effortless recall.

To use this system, simply assign the appropriate letters to the number you wish to memorize. For example, my phone number is 714-833-8258.

THE PHONETIC CODE SYSTEM

NUMBER	CODE	EXPLANATION
0	s, z, and soft c.	"Zero" has almost the same sound as these letters.
1	t, d, th	The letters "t" and "d" both have one downstroke. "Th" has a similar sound to these letters.
2	n	The letter "n" has two downstrokes
3	m	"M" has three downstrokes.
4	r	"R" is the last letter in the word "four."
5	l	The capital letter L is the Roman numeral for 50.
6	j, ch, sh, soft g, & dg	The letter "j" is the mirror image of the digit 6; the other letter combinations all have basically the same sound.
7	k, hard c, q & hard g,	The written capital "K" looks like a seven
8	f, v, & ph	The cursive "f" in script looks like an 8.
9	p & b	The letter "p" is the mirror image of the digit 9; and the letter "b" is an inverted "p".

The letter codes for this number could be: GTR-FMM-FNLV. A word substitution for this could be *Guitar-Foam-Fun-Love*. To remember this, see me having a great time playing a foam rubber guitar. Remember that the guitar has an M&M stuck to it, and you'll remember that foam (FMM) has two m's. If you want to attach this number to my name, see the foam guitar sticking out of an ice cream cone, and see me having fun because I love eating ice cream.

THE PEG SYSTEM

The *peg system* is an extension of the phonetic code system. It is composed of ninety-nine words that use the letters in the phonetic code. Using the peg system involves memorizing the pegs. This is not as hard as it seems if you already know the phonetic coding system previously discussed in this chapter. Each word begins with its phonetic code letter. For instance, the first word begins with a "t" which is associated with the number 1. The two digit numbers use two code letters. The list of 99 words I have provided on page 103 is widely used, but you can make up your own words if you prefer.

You can use the peg system to memorize lists of items by attaching each item to its peg word.

For example, let's go back to the list we used for the locus system.

1. broccoli
2. lettuce
3. mayonnaise
4. hot dogs
5. peanut butter
6. potato chips
7. tomatoes
8. hamburger
9. a copy of the *Enquirer*
10. a jar of mustard

To use the peg system, attach each item to a numbered peg word. See a stalk of broccoli wearing your favorite tie. Now get a picture of Noah chewing on a head of lettuce. See your "ma" spreading mayonnaise on a sandwich (remember that Mayonnaise begins with "ma") and put the hot dogs on rye.

Now see yourself breaking the law by throwing a jar of peanut butter through a window. Then you get a cramp in your jaw from eating a whole bag of potato chips. You shove your car key through a tomato, and throw a pound of hamburger at someone you hate (a foe). You then catch your "pa" actually reading a copy of the *Enquirer,* and cover his toes with mustard.

Stop for a moment now, close your eyes and remember the words.

If you've formed the links properly, the words will come immediately to mind.

THE 99 PEG WORDS

1. tie	34. mower	67. chalk
2. Noah	35. mule	68. chef
3. ma	36. match	69. ship
4. rye	37. mug	70. case
5. law	38. movie	71. cot
6. jaw	39. mop	72. can
7. key	40. rose	73. comb
8. foe	41. rat	74. car
9. pa	42. rain	75. coal
10. toes	43. ram	76. cage
11. tot	44. rower	77. coke
12. tin	45. roll	78. cave
13. tomb	46. roach	79. cob
14. tire	47. rock	80. fuse
15. towel	48. roof	81. fat
16. dish	49. rope	82. fan
17. dog	50. lace	83. foam
18. dove	51. lad	84. fur
19. tub	52. lane	85. file
20. nose	53. lamb	86. fish
21. net	54. lair	87. fog
22. nun	55. lily	88. fife
23. name	56. leech	89. fob
24. Nero	57. log	90. bus
25. nail	58. lava	91. bat
26. notch	59. lip	92. bone
27. neck	60. cheese	93. bum
28. knife	61. sheet	94. bear
29. knob	62. chain	95. bell
30. mouse	63. chime	96. beach
31. mat	64. cherry	97. book
32. money	65. jail	98. puff
33. mummy	66. cha-cha	99. pipe

CHAPTER TEN

BIOLOGICAL RHYTHM AND MEMORY

My aunt Lucille could tell herself to wake up anytime of the day or night. She could say she would be up at 6:52, and when the time arrived, her eyes would open. People like Aunt Lucille who can do this have learned to pay attention to the subtle cues from by their biological clock.

All living things have a biological clock within them, and human beings are no exception. In concert with the earth's rotation, we exhibit a daily rhythm known as *circadian rhythm.* The word "circadian" comes from the Latin term "circa dies," which means "about a day."

Each day, our bodies go through a complex biological cycle which alters moods, tastes, opinions, and beliefs—how we see the world at ten o'clock in the morning is much different than the way we see it at ten at night.

This rhythm also alters our tolerance for foods and drugs, and this is why cocktail hour is in the evening. The body has a much greater tolerance for alcohol in the evening than it does in the morning. This circadian rhythm is also why certain foods taste better in the morning than at night, and why we have specific foods for breakfast, lunch and dinner. For example, cereal, pancakes, and eggs are breakfast foods, while pasta is not.

For most of us, this rhythm begins at a low point in the morning when we first awaken, and reaches a peak some time in mid morning. We then experience a slump in midday, usually somewhere between noon and three in the afternoon. We reach another energy peak in mid-evening, and then our energy decreases steadily until bedtime.

These rhythms fall into two categories, one with its highest peak in the morning, and the other with its highest peak in the evening. People who have a high energy peak in the morning are of course called "morning people," and people who have their highest peak in the evening are called "night people." You are probably aware of your own type of rhythm.

Morning people wake up immediately, feeling rested and energetic. They do their best work before noon. They are tired by the end of the day, and are not much interested in night life.

Night people, on the other hand, find it difficult to wake up in the morning. It sometimes takes them several hours to really get going. They find that they do their best work in the evening, and usually enjoy staying up late.

This rhythm also modifies our ability to remember. Our ability to put things into and get things out of our memory depends on our personal biological rhythm. If you are a morning person, your ability to learn is greater in the morning, and if you are a night person, it is greater in the evening.

Almost all of us experience a midday slump, the time of day where we feel tired and foggy-minded, and this time of day is not a good time to memorize new material, hold an important meeting, or take a class.

As memory is a function of our ability to focus, we find it more difficult to remember things that were experienced during this time period.

Becoming aware of your own biological rhythm will help you increase your ability to learn and remember. Choose your peak time of day to learn new material.

Don't attempt memorization when you're tired. Your stimulus filters do not work well at these times, and easy tasks seem overwhelming when you are exhausted. However, it helps to review study material right before bedtime, because the information is stored during your dreams.

ULTRADIAN RHYTHM

The human cerebral cortex (the outer layer of the brain) consists of two identical looking hemispheres. In 1972, a series of studies done by researchers Goldstein, Stoltzfus and Gardocki demonstrated that the cerebral hemispheres alternate in dominance on a 90 minute cycle. This cycle is akin to the 90-minute sleep cycle and is known as *ultradian rhythm*. Two other brain researchers, Klein and Armitage, discovered in 1979 that the 90 minute oscillations actually affected cognitive style and mental activity.

Then, in 1981, Debra Werntz found that the 90-minute rhythm was associated with the nasal breathing cycle. When the left nostril is open, the right hemisphere of the brain is dominant. Further research demonstrated that cerebral dominance could be altered by changing the nasal breathing pattern. Psychologist Ernest Rossi found that one way to do this is to lie on your side—lying on your left side activates the left hemisphere because the right nostril is open.

Because the hemispheres differ in the type of information they store and process, it is possible to increase access to the information by activating the proper hemisphere.

These findings suggest that ultradian rhythm is one explanation of the "tip of the tongue" phenomenon. As discussed earlier, this is the temporary inability to retrieve information from memory, even though we are sure we know it. Waiting a short period of time, or closing one nostril for a few minutes allows the brain to shift hemispheres, and access the desired information.

CHAPTER ELEVEN

SLEEP, DREAMING AND MEMORY

Sleep Requirements

A good night's sleep is something that everyone desires. Each of us is born with a requirement for a certain amount of sleep. While some can get by with just three or four hours sleep per night, others need as much as ten hours per night in order to feel rested. It is a popular myth in our culture that everyone needs eight hours sleep to stay healthy.

Here is how it breaks down statistically. About 80% of Americans doze an average of 7.5 hours per night, while another 15% need only 6.5 hours of sleep to feel rested. About 1% of the population requires less than 5 hours of sleep per night, while another 1% actually needs up to 10 hours.

If you are convinced that you should get eight hours of rest every night, but your body actually needs ten hours, you will be constantly depriving your body of the sleep it needs. This will result in being perpetually fatigued. Fatigue lowers your tolerance for frustration, and impairs your ability to concentrate. In addition, when you're tired your stimulus filters don't work which will make you easily distracted.

On the other hand, if you are a person who actually requires only four hours of slumber to feel rested, but you force yourself to sleep longer, you will upset your natural biological rhythm. This will decrease your ability to concentrate.

Recent studies have reinforced the old adage "early to bed and early to rise." Subjects who went to bed an hour earlier than their normal bed time and awoke at their regular time showed an increased ability to concentrate the next day. This was seen as evidence that these people were chronically depriving themselves of sleep by staying awake too late, and then forcing themselves to awaken each morning by the sound of an alarm clock.

Studies on modern American lifestyle indicate that many of us are short-changing ourselves on sleep by staying up late and then forcing ourselves to get up before we are rested. In his book *Sleep Thieves* researcher Stanley Coren concurred and reported that even one hour of increased sleep at night can improve your memory. Several sleep and memory studies suggest that a person who gets enough sleep does not need an alarm to wake them.

Sleep Problems

As we age, we naturally need less sleep. In addition, it's common for older people to wake up several times during the night. While less sleep and nighttime awakenings are normal, many people worry about this, and begin to believe that they have insomnia.

Insomnia is by far the most common complaint about sleep, and about half of the population over 50 complain about sleep problems. There are three basic types of insomnia. The first is called *sleep onset insomnia*, and is characterized by the inability to fall asleep. People with this type of insomnia may lie in bed for over an hour before falling asleep.

The second type is *sleep maintenance insomnia*, characterized by the inability to stay asleep. People suffering from this type of insomnia may wake up many times a night.

The third type is *early morning awakening*, in which the person awakens before they wish to, and cannot return to sleep.

Another common and potentially dangerous sleep problem is *sleep apnea*. This is caused by an obstruction in the air flow during sleep. A person suffering from apnea may actually stop breathing for more than a minute. Most people with sleep apnea snore, and sleep poorly. During the day they are fatigued and listless. Fortunately this condition can usually be remedied with minor surgery.

To sleep, perchance to remember?

So why is sleep important to memory?

First, sleeping *too much* can impair memory. As mentioned above, as people age, they need less sleep. In a recent report, a 59- year old retired physician came to a clinic for medical help because of mental confusion. It was found that the cause of the problem was merely that he was sleeping too much. When his sleep time was temporarily reduced to 3 hours 45 minutes, the confusion cleared. One treatment for depression involves keeping people awake for extended periods of time. Like the gentleman just mentioned, depressed people often sleep too much.

Second, dreaming is essential to memory. During slumber, the body goes through a cycle consisting of alternate periods of light sleep, deep sleep, and another type of sleep called *rapid eye movement* or REM sleep. We do much of our dreaming during REM sleep.

While in REM, hands and feet may twitch, and eyes dart around under eyelids. If you have ever watched someone else sleep, you may have seen this happening.

Studies on sleep and memory show that information gathered during the day is categorized and stored in long term memory during REM sleep. If you are a person who remembers dreams, you might have noticed that the activities of the previous day show up in your dreams. Dream theorists call this the *day residue*.

In 1978, Howard Roffwarg conducted a fascinating study which helped explain how day residue is incorporated into our dreams and our memory. During the day, nine college students wore special goggles that colored everything red. After a few hours, the subjects soon became acclimated to a "goggle-colored" world. On the day that they started wearing the lenses, all of their visual input was "tagged" with color.

Roffwarg reasoned that whatever information was processed during REM sleep would include the colored goggle world input. Each night the subjects slept in a sleep lab, where their EEGs and eye movements were monitored. They were awakened during REM sleep and asked to report their dreams. The subjects experienced four REM periods each night. On the first night, goggle material began to enter their dreams, but only during the first REM period.

In the subjects' first dream of the night, about half of the scenes contained red information. On succeeding nights, however, red scenes appeared in later and later dream periods. By the fifth night scenes from all REM periods contained goggle-colored material. As the red color moved into later dreams, it also increased in the first dream period, so that by the fifth night the first REM period contained 83% red scenes.

This study suggests that material appearing in dreams later in the night comes from earlier memories, which suggests that past material is mixed with recent material during sleep. In this way we weave present experiences to past memories which gives our life a sense of continuity.

Since it appears that memory is categorized and stored during REM sleep, lack of REM means impaired memory storage. For this reason, it's important that you get adequate amounts of REM each night.

Most sleeping medications on the market today prevent you from getting adequate REM sleep. Alcohol can also have this effect. If you are taking sleeping pills on a regular basis, or if you drink every night. you are impairing your ability to store information in your long-term memory. If you are having trouble sleeping at night, it is a good idea to find the cause of your insomnia, and correct that problem, rather than drugging yourself to sleep.

If you have been taking sleeping medication for some time, do not attempt to stop without consulting your doctor. Sudden withdrawal from sleeping medication can cause serious health problems.

If you are having trouble sleeping try the following:

•   Establish a regular sleep schedule. Go to bed and get up the same time each day, including weekends.

•   Establish a regular routine of exercise. Exercise is one of the most effective remedies for insomnia. (Do not exercise right before bedtime, as the simulation will keep you awake.)

- Get exposure to sunlight each day. If you can't do that, get some natural light bulbs, which mimic the effects of sunlight. Sunlight helps regulate your biological clock.

- Avoid caffeine and other stimulants. Caffeine takes a long time to metabolize. A cup of coffee in the morning may actually be keeping you awake that night.

- Don't use alcohol to help you sleep. Alcohol causes insomnia, especially sleep maintenance insomnia.

- Develop a bedtime ritual. Do the same things each night before bedtime, as this will cue your body that it's time to sleep. Use your bed only for sleeping. This makes getting into bed a sleeping cue.

For more information about sleep problems, contact the Better Sleep Council, PO Box 13, Washington DC 20044. Also write to the Wakefulness-Sleep Education & Research Foundation, 4820 Rancho Drive, Del Mar CA 92014, and ask for information about purchasing *101 Questions About Sleep and Dreams*.

And for those who want further reading, the American Association of Retired Persons, 601 E Street, NW, Washington, DC 20049, publishes *The Sleep Book*.

CHAPTER TWELVE

BRAIN FUNCTION AND BLOOD FLOW

Although the brain weighs in at only 2% of our body weight, it consumes 20% of the oxygen we use. In children, the oxygen use of the brain can actually be as high as 50%.

Doctors calculate the overall oxygen absorption in the body by using a measure called $VO2_{max}$. $VO2_{max}$ is highest in adolescence, and declines with age. In adults, $VO2_{max}$ declines about 1% a year, and decreases about 23% between the ages of 33 and 61.

The brain cannot store oxygen. Because of this, it must rely on a constant supply of oxygen delivered through the blood stream. A decrease in oxygen dispensed to the brain results in an immediate impairment in brain function, and a change in blood supply is felt almost instantly. You may have experienced how fast a drop in blood flow can affect your consciousness if you have ever stood up too fast.

In healthy people, the total blood flow to the brain is remarkably constant. The blood supply to the brain doesn't significantly increase during exercise, and doesn't drastically decrease during inactivity or sleep. Normal blood flow to the brain is about 50_{ml} per minute. Slight fluctuations may go unnoticed, but if the flow of blood is decreased to 30_{ml} per minute, mental confusion and even loss of consciousness may occur.

In a healthy, middle-aged person, a drop of blood pressure below normal usually has no effect, but in an elderly person the brain is especially dependent on a strong blood supply. If blood flow is reduced too much, the brain cells become starved for oxygen, causing an impairment in thinking, or in extreme cases, a stroke. A chronic lack of oxygen to the brain can cause confusion and symptoms of senility.

WATER LEVEL

The amount of water stored in the body has an important effect on the brain's blood supply. In younger people, water balance is maintained adequately, but as we age the total amount of body fluids decreases. Body water level actually falls from 62% at the age of 25, to 50% at the age of 75. This lower fluid level means that there is less room for altering body water levels without affecting brain function.

To make matters worse, many older people decrease their fluid intake, because they have lost their taste for liquids and because they simply forget to drink enough water. In addition, older people avoid drinking fluids because it increases their need to urinate.

Because the fluid levels are lower in elderly people, the circulatory system becomes extremely sensitive to changes of both water and salt levels in the body. *Diuretics*, which are drugs used to lower blood pressure, reduce the body's salt and water levels. If the dosage of these drugs is too high, the drugs may lower blood pressure to such a degree that the fluid level of the body becomes dangerously low.

Although it is not often pointed out by doctors, one of the most common side effects of blood pressure medication in the elderly is memory loss.

THE ARTERIES

The blood vessels that supply oxygen to the body are called *arteries*. The wall of an artery consists of several layers of smooth muscle. Arteries actually manufacture cholesterol, but at the same time prevent the cholesterol from accumulating on the surface of their walls.

Blood is supplied to the human brain by four major arteries. The two *internal carotid arteries* supply about 85% of total blood flow to the brain. The *vertebral arteries* supply the remaining 15%. If these vessels become blocked or clogged with plaque, blood flow to the brain is diminished, and this condition must be corrected to restore proper brain nourishment.

THE CAROTID ARTERIES

Two large arteries, called the *carotid arteries*, supply blood to the cerebral hemispheres. There is one carotid on each side of the neck.

A small branch of the carotid supplies blood to the artery of the eye. If this branch of the carotid artery becomes narrowed by atherosclerosis, and part of the plaque breaks off and travels to the brain, the afflicted person may experience a temporary loss of vision to one eye. People who have experienced this describe it as having a curtain drawn in front of their eye. These episodes may occur several times a day.

People over 40, particularly if they have diabetes or high blood pressure, should have their carotid arteries checked regularly. Your doctor can diagnose whether narrowing of the carotid artery has occurred through the use of a stethoscope. If a murmur (called a *bruit*) is heard over the carotid artery in the middle of the upper portion of the neck, narrowing has occurred. More sophisticated testing includes X rays with the use of dye, and computer analysis. The most recent technique for diagnosing carotid narrowing is sonar examination.

Blockage of the carotids is serious. If the carotid artery becomes so blocked that blood flow to the brain is impaired, surgery may be required. The operation, called an *endarterectomy*, is similar to roto-rootering the artery. If the damage to the artery is severe, doctors may replace a portion of it with a vessel from another part of the body, often from the leg.

Some doctors claim that neurological deficits and cognitive functioning improve after the procedure, because of improved blood flow to areas of the brain which were impaired before the operation. If the blockage is not too severe, aspirin can sometimes be used as a substitute for this surgery, because it impedes the formation of blood clots.

THE BASILAR ARTERY

At the base of the brain is the *basilar artery*. This artery furnishes the brain stem and the merging cranial nerves with blood. Patients with atherosclerosis in the basilar artery complain of vertigo and nausea. Vertigo is the very unpleasant feeling of spinning around in space. Often the person has the feeling that everything around him is spinning uncontrollably. This feeling can be very uncomfortable, and can sometimes cause vomiting.

Patients with blockage in the basilar artery frequently complain of having tingling sensations around their mouth, and may have difficulty pronouncing words. They may also have swallowing problems.

When the blood flow through this artery is interrupted, the person may suffer a brief loss of consciousness, or may fall down. There may also be a loss of equilibrium, staggering, and behavior that mimics drunkenness. Some people with this problem are not able to walk at all.

Many of these symptoms can also be caused by an infection of the inner ear, and should not be confused with basilar artery problems. Also, a rare congenital disorder called Arnold-Chiari's malformation has been known to cause similar symptoms. These things should be ruled out before basilar artery damage is considered.

ATHEROSCLEROSIS

As we age, the blood flow to our brain decreases. Often this is caused by the blockage of blood flow in the arteries themselves.

The medical term for any type of hardening of the arteries is *arteriosclerosis*. *Atherosclerosis* is a form of arteriosclerosis in which the layers of the artery become thickened and irregular. This gradual blockage is caused by debris, by deposits of cholesterol, and by other fatty deposits that build up in the arterial wall, just as sludge builds up in a drainpipe. These deposits narrow the arteries and impede blood flow. The medical term for these deposits is *atheromas*.

Clogged arteries and capillaries cannot deliver adequate oxygen and nutrients to the brain cells. And as a result, the brain cannot function properly.

Normally the arterial walls are smooth and clean, but high blood pressure puts stress on the arterial walls, which can cause small tears in the arterial surface. Cholesterol collects in these tiny tears. Once this process has begun, the cholesterol builds up into hard deposits called *plaque*.

As this process progresses, the artery becomes thick and hard and loses its elasticity. A diseased artery can actually change from the consistency of a rubber hose to that of a hard, plastic pipe.

The process of arterial blockage begins much earlier than you might think. In fact, many people begin developing blockage by age 15. Medical tests show that in most people over 20, the *intima* and the *media*, the inner and middle layers of the arteries, have already begun to become packed with cholesterol.

Plaque can form in any artery, but it is particularly dangerous when it collects in the arteries in the brain, where the buildup can lead to strokes, or in the coronary arteries, which can cause heart attacks.

CHOLESTEROL

Cholesterol level plays a crucial part in atherosclerosis. Buildup of plaque generally begins to occur in the brain when blood cholesterol is above 260_{mg}. The higher your serum cholesterol, the greater your risk of developing atherosclerosis. In fact, people with cholesterol above 260_{mg}. have a three to five times greater chance of developing arterial clots than people with cholesterol below 200.

You can measure your propensity towards atherosclerosis through a blood test. The blood test will measure cholesterol, triglycerides, high density lipoprotein (HDL), and low density lipoprotein (LDL).

While most of the cholesterol in our bodies is actually manufactured by the liver, 20 or 30% of it comes from dietary sources, and we now know that arteriosclerosis can be slowed, stopped, and can even be reversed through dietary modification.

FOODS AND NUTRIENTS THAT
LOWER CHOLESTEROL

A glass of red wine a day	Two carrots a day
	Grapefruit
Two apples a day	Garlic and onions
High fiber diet	Vitamin C & E
Pectin	Coenzyme Q_{10}
Lecithin	Evening Primrose Oil
Skim milk	Niacin
Lemon grass	Chromium
Cold water fish	Folic acid
Soy products	Omega-3 fatty acids
Beans	L-Carnitine

Although there is a lot of controversy about how dietary cholesterol affects atherosclerosis, it's generally agreed that the less cholesterol in the diet, the lower the risk of atherosclerosis. Dr. Dean Ornish in his book, *Eat More, Weigh Less*, has shown that eating a no-fat diet can prevent, and in some cases actually reverse cardiovascular disease.

For information on lowering your cholesterol, contact the National Cholesterol Education Program (NCEP), National Heart, Lung, and Blood Institute, NHLB Information Center, 4733 Bethesda Avenue, Suite 530, Bethesda, MD 20814-4820. Telephone (301) 951-3260. Another source of information is the Consumer Nutrition Hotline at (800) 366-1655.

For information about the new synthetic fat substitutes on the market, request *Sorting Out the Facts about Fat*, Publications Department, IFIC, Food Education Foundation, 1100 Connecticut Avenue NW, Suite 430, Washington, DC 20036. The phone number for the International Food Information Council (IFIC) is (202) 296-6540.

TRANSIENT ISCHEMIC ATTACKS

Tiny strokes, called *transient ischemic attacks* (TIAs), mimic strokes in their symptoms, causing numbness, nausea and dizziness. But unlike actual strokes, which can cause permanent disability, TIAs last only up to 24 hours. TIAs are caused by a temporary decrease in the blood flow to different parts of the brain. When this occurs, there's often a loss of motor ability and thinking capacity that lasts several minutes to a day, and then disappears.

The major cause of TIAs is atherosclerosis of the arteries supplying the brain. Other less common causes include episodes of irregular heartbeats, low blood pressure and brain tumors.

If the blood flow to a part of the brain called the hippocampus is blocked during a TIA, memory loss will occur. Repeated episodes of TIAs over time may cause dementia.

Other symptoms of TIAs include brief flashes of numbness in the face and the arms, or sudden weakness of an arm or a leg with the inability to move.

Having a TIA is a very terrifying experience, but between these little attacks, the sufferer feels fine. For this reason, people often fail to go to the doctor to have them checked out.

Even though people with TIAs may have no signs of heart disease, they should have a thorough cardiac workup, because many also have hardening in the arteries of the heart. In fact, the cause of death in people with TIAs is usually heart attack.

In 1978, the Mayo Clinic reported that one-third of patients with TIAs will suffer a stroke within five years of the first attack. Twenty per-cent will suffer stroke within one month of the initial attack, and 50% within a year. As we shall see, strokes can be devastating and sometimes fatal events. But they are, in part, preventable.

STROKE

A *stroke* is the destruction of brain cells caused by an interruption of blood flow to the brain. Strokes are the leading source of adult disability, and the number three cause of death (after heart disease and cancer). They afflict about 500,000 Americans each year.

THE MAJOR CAUSES OF STROKE
High blood pressure
Heart disease
High cholesterol
Overweight
Smoking
Alcohol
Lack of exercise
Diabetes

Eighty percent of stroke victims survive, but they often suffer permanent loss of function, such as the loss of the ability to speak (called *aphasia*) or paralysis of part of the body. Strokes are also called *cerebral vascular accidents* (CVAs) but they are, in fact, not accidents; to a great degree, they can be predicted and prevented.

The number of strokes in the United States has decreased almost 50% in the last thirty years. This is attributed primarily to the medical control of high blood pressure. Still, almost a half million people a year in the United States suffer from strokes.

Researchers have found that a brain chemical called *calpain* may cause brain cell damage after a stroke. Normally calpain cleans up blocked receptors in neurons and facilitates memory transfer, but too much calpain in the system kills neurons.

When a stroke occurs, it is followed by the release of glutamate, a chemical that causes brain damage. This phenomenon is called a *glutamate cascade*.

Some researchers believe that *Dextromethorphan*, a substance found in most cough syrups, can protect the brain against stroke damage. In animals, high doses of the drug administered after a brain injury reduced damage by 80%. It reduced brain swelling by 85%.

It has also been found that *nitric oxide*, a substance released by glutamate, can cause stroke damage. FK 506, an experimental immuno-suppressant drug, blocks nitric oxide, and therefore may reduce stroke damage.

Strokes occur in three major ways. As mentioned earlier, *plaque* is the debris that blocks arteries in atherosclerosis. A blood clot that completely clogs an artery and causes a stroke is called a *thrombus,* and the incident is called a thrombic stroke. When a bit of plaque, called an *embolus* breaks off and clogs a smaller vessel or capillary, it is called an *embolic stroke.* When an artery in the brain actually bursts, and spills blood on the brain, the incident is called a *hemorrhagic stroke.* This type of stroke usually occurs from a combination of atherosclerosis and high blood pressure. About 80% of strokes are of the thrombic type.

In the past few years, it's been discovered that injections of a clot-dissolving drug called *tissue plasminogen activator* (TPA) can dramatically improve the chances of stroke patients recovering with few lasting effects. In a study of 624 stroke patients, victims were randomly assigned to get either TPA or a placebo. After three months, doctors judged the patients' conditions on four scales of stroke symptoms. Depending on the measure used, those getting TPA were between 30% and 50% more likely to have full or nearly complete recoveries.

On the most conservative of these scales, the doctors found that 31% of the patients receiving TPA showed no permanent disability, or were left with minor symptoms such as slight weakness in one arm. By comparison, only 20% of those in the untreated group were this fortunate.

TPA is not a cure-all. To be effective, it must be administered within the first three hours of the onset of symptoms. Furthermore, all patients must be given a CAT scan first to make sure that the stroke is from a blood clot in the brain and not from a broken blood vessel. Since prompt treatment is essential, strokes are know considered emergencies by ambulance crews and hospitals.

TPA does carry a high level of risk. Giving TPA too late in the course of a stroke may trigger bleeding in the brain, causing further damage. Theses hazards were illustrated by a major study in which European doctors gave TPA to patients six hours after stroke symptoms began. Among victims who already had large areas of drying brain tissue, TPA increased the risk of death by two-thirds.

Even when the drug is used properly, it increases bleeding in the brain in 6% of patients. However, the study concludes that this hazard is offset by the reduction in symptoms among stroke survivors. When given to the right person at the right time, it can prevent lifelong disability.

BLACK TEA AND STROKE

According to an article in the March 25 issue of the *Archives of Internal Medicine*, regular, long-term consumption of black tea, and other substances containing a family of chemicals called *flavonoids* may protect against stroke.

Sirving O. Keli, M.D., Ph.D. and his colleagues studied 552 men, aged 50 to 69 years, between 1970 and 1985, to test a theory that the dietary antioxidant vitamins and flavonoids in fruits and vegetables shield against stroke. The major source of flavonoids consumed was from Black tea (70%), while apples contributed about 10%.

The study showed an inverse association between tea consumption and stroke risk. Men who drank more than 4.7 cups of tea per day actually had a 69% reduced risk of stroke compared with men who drank less than 2.6 cups per day. Tea also contains other antioxidative compounds which may contribute to this effect.

The researchers concluded that,"long-term intake of flavonoids and consumption of black tea may protect against stroke."

In addition to black tea and apples, onions, kale, green beans, broccoli, endive, celery and cranberries all contain high levels of flavonoids.

For more information about strokes, contact the American Heart Association, 7272 Greenville Avenue, Dallas TX 75231, Telephone (800) 242-8721. Or call the National Stroke Association, 96 Inverness Drive, East, Suite I, Englewood, CO 80112. Telephone (800) STR-OKES or (303) 649-9299.

MAXIMIZING BLOOD FLOW

It's clear that healthy arteries and unimpeded bloodflow are vital to proper brain function. Fortunately, scientists have found several ways to increase blood flow to the brain, and reduce the risk of stroke.

Numerous studies have demonstrated that exercise slightly increases brain blood flow. However, even this small rise is enough to improve mental abilities. These studies show that people who make even a modest effort do better at memorizing and processing information than those who have not increase their activity level.

Exercise also helps to reduce the stress and tension in your body, and enhances your ability to concentrate. In general, the more physically active you are, the better your brain works.

Some studies show that exercising at least three times a week can increase brain oxygen uptake by as much as 30%.

Exercise also can affect cholesterol levels. There are two types of cholesterol. LDL (bad cholesterol) causes heart attacks, whereas HDL (good cholesterol) actually protects you from heart attacks. The goal is to keep LDL down, while maintaining high HDL levels.

In a recent study done at Stanford University, 377 men and women with moderately high LDL (bad) cholesterol and moderately low amounts of HDL (good) cholesterol, who added an exercise program to a low-fat diet plan for one year lowered LDL cholesterol two times as much as did people who used diet alone.

Women who added exercise to low-fat eating lowered their LDL about 12 mg./dl. more than people who did nothing. Men on the same program lowered LDL by about 15 mg./dl. more than those who did not change their habits. Eating less than 25% of calories from fat without exercising changed LDL only about 5 to 6 mg./dl. for both men and women. It's important to note that exercise alone had no effect on cholesterol levels. Both exercise and fat reduction are necessary to get a significant result.

It is thought that exercise lowers LDL by facilitating weight loss. Abdominal fat in particular is a problem because the blood circulating through it drains directly into the liver. The liver, receiving fat-laden blood from the abdomen, then manufactures LDL. When abdominal fat is reduced, the liver has less raw material with which to create LDL. Studies show that staying at your ideal weight is linked to lower LDL.

A study from Barcelona looked at HDL (good) choles-terol. Of 537 men studied, those who worked out for 15 minutes at a rate of 420 calories per hour had HDL levels about 2 mg./dl. higher than those who worked out at a more moderate rate.

A study published in *Medicine and Science in Sports and Exercise* demonstrated that exercise also sharpened brain function. In this study 32 subjects were given a battery of tests for mental function. They then took a ten week program in physical fitness. When they were tested again, there was a significant improvement in intelligence. This means exercise alone increased their I.Q.!

The *American Psychologist* reported that people over 60 who took a daily stroll of 6 to 10 miles experienced increased brain function in only 26 days. In another study, reported in the journal *Psychosomatic Medicine,* college students who attended a 14-week swimming class reported less tension, depression, and confusion. Various measurements showed that swimming increased blood flow, oxygen uptake, and availability of nutrients to the brain.

There is another reason why the activity of swimming brings brain benefits. Researcher Win Younger suggests that holding your breath under water increases the amount of blood that travels to the brain by expanding the carotid arteries. If the swimming routine is performed regularly, the increase can become permanent, which can improve mental capacity.

As mentioned above, cleaning out the carotid arteries through surgery removes plaque, but it's been shown that certain tropical fruits help tidy up the arteries too. Bananas, kiwis, papayas and mangoes all contain *bromelian*, a substance that keeps arteries clean.

Grapefruit and apple pectin also help by lowering cholesterol. One study demonstrated that eating 12 grams of grapefruit pectin a day over four months brought down cholesterol by 17%. You can buy grapefruit pectin in health food stores in tablet form. One gram of vitamin C per day can also lower your cholesterol.

Several studies show that thyroid imbalance can affect the condition of your arteries. William Kountz found that 288 low-thyroid patients all had high cholesterol. Stephen Langer in his book, *Solved: The Riddle of Illness*, suggests that a kelp tablet a day can balance the thyroid in many people.

COFFEE AND CHOLESTEROL

There are several studies that suggest moderate to heavy coffee drinking can cause a significant rise in cholesterol levels. Norwegian researchers examined the relation between coffee consumption and levels of total serum cholesterol, high-density -lipoprotein (HDL) cholesterol, and triglycerides in a population of 7,213 women and 7,368 men between the ages of 20 and 54. They found that moderate coffee drinkers (those drinking four cups or less a day) had cholesterol levels 5% higher than non-coffee-drinkers.

People who drank five to eight cups a day had cholesterol levels 9% higher, and those who drank more than nine cups of coffee per day had cholesterol levels 12% higher than non-coffee-drinkers. The researchers stated, "...the present finding of a coffee-cholesterol association ... is strong and consistent, and its magnitude makes coffee one of the strongest determinants of serum cholesterol levels in the present population."

Researchers at Stanford University also studied the effects of coffee on "bad" LDL cholesterol and apolipoprotein B (apo-B), a fat molecule which attaches itself to protein. In this study, male university employees between the ages of 30 and 55 who drank more than 2½ to 3 cups per day had elevated plasma concentrations of three cardiovascular risk factors: total cholesterol, LDL cholesterol, and apo-B.

At the University of Texas, researchers also found a coffee -cholesterol link. In their study, serum cholesterol rose from 205.3mg/dl in women who drank less than a cup of coffee a day to 223.1mg/dl among those who drank eight or more cups. Serum cholesterol in men rose from 206.7mg/dl for those who consumed less than a cup of coffee daily to 226.5mg/dl among those who downed eight or more cups.

Researchers are not sure how coffee drinking or associated factors spur this increase in cholesterol. Neither the cream in the coffee, nor stress, nor cigarettes appear to be behind this cholesterol effect. It isn't the caffeine either. Researchers looked at tea and cola drinkers but did not find increases in cholesterol.

In a 30 year study at Johns Hopkins, published in the *New England Journal of Medicine* in 1986, subjects who consumed five or more cups of coffee per day had the highest cumulative incidence of coronary artery disease (10.7%). This group of coffee drinkers was compared with subjects who drank three to four cups a day (8.8% were found to have heart disease), one to two cups per day (a 5.1 % finding), or no coffee (a 1.6 % incidence).

Several recent studies have failed to replicate these results, so the coffee cholesterol link remains controversial. Other studies show that if the coffee is filtered, the toxic components are eliminated. Even though the evidence is conflicting, those with high cholesterol might quit coffee for a while to see if it helps.

Coffee can also cause irregular heart beats and several studies have demonstrated a significant increase in blood pressure after drinking a cup. Go easy on coffee.

CHELATION THERAPY

Chelation therapy utilizes a substance called *ethylene diamine tetra acetic acid* (EDTA). This is a protein like molecule that binds to metal ions such as lead, mercury and calcium, and makes them soluble in the blood. This allows the kidney to eliminate heavy metals from the body. Chelation therapy has been the treatment of choice for heavy metal poisoning for years.

Dr. Norman Clark began researching chelation therapy in the early 1950's. He felt that because calcium was deposited in cholesterol plaques that plugged arteries, it made good sense that EDTA, which removes calcium, could soften the plaques and lead to a reversal of the cholesterol deposits. When he began to use the treatment for this purpose, Dr. Clark found that infusions of EDTA improved symptoms in as much as 80% of his patients.

Since that time, traditional medicine has decided that chelation therapy is an ineffective treatment for unclogging arteries. But even though most doctors claim that chelation is worthless, there are several hundred physicians in the U.S. that swear by it as an effective cure for cardiovascular disease, and to reverse some symptoms of dementia.

For more information on chelation therapy, and a list of physicians in your area who use it, contact the American College of Advancement in Medicine (ACAM) at (714) 583-7666.

CHAPTER THIRTEEN

BLOOD PRESSURE

LOW BLOOD PRESSURE

Low blood pressure is more common than suspected, and causes many problems with memory, thinking, and concentration. Low blood pressure can be caused by chronic blood loss, inadequate fluid intake, excessive vomiting, heart attacks, heat exhaustion, endocrine diseases and abnormalities in thyroid function.

The medical term for low blood pressure is *hypotension* In elderly people, low blood pressure is responsible for a variety of brain problems.

The *hippocampus*, which is a part of the brain that allows us to store memories, is notoriously prone to damage from insufficient blood supply, inadequate oxygen levels, or deficits in nutrients.

Because of the odd geometry of its blood vessels, the hippocampus is highly prone to deterioration from hardening of the arteries. Low blood pressure can damage this delicate tissue and cause permanent memory problems. For this reason, maintaining adequate fluid intake is essential.

Some of my patients with low blood pressure either have congestive heart failure or medication problems. In cases of medication issues, often when the person stops taking the problem-causing drug, their blood pressure returns to normal.

HIGH BLOOD PRESSURE

High blood pressure is also known as *hypertension.* Basically in cases of hypertension, the tension inside the blood vessels is too high. Some people get confused and wrongly think that hypertension means that you are more tense emotionally than you should be.

We've known for years that high blood pressure is a major factor in the acceleration of arteriosclerosis. When high blood pressure is decreased, the incidence of strokes, atherosclerosis and dementia is greatly reduced.

Researchers have found that men with high blood pressure are significantly slower in searching their short-term memory than are men with normal blood pressure. The authors of this study believe that decreases in cerebral blood flow could be the cause. Many other studies show that untreated high blood pressure does indeed impair memory.

At least 35 million people in the United States are known to have hypertension. Most are unaware that they have it. High blood pressure usually has no symptoms, and therefore is has come to be known as the *silent killer.*

High blood pressure affects over 20% of the adult white population in the United States and over 30% of the adult black population.

However, in higher age groups, these percentages increase significantly. About two-thirds of the people between ages 65 and 74, and three-fourths of the people over 75 have high blood pressure.

Even though high blood pressure usually has no symptoms, there may be some warning signs. These include a rapid pulse, feelings of dizziness, chronic headaches, sweating, problems with vision, and shortness of breath.

There are many ways to lower blood pressure without medication. However, before you try any of them, heed the following words of caution.

All of the information in this chapter has been gathered from research studies, magazine articles, and books on blood pressure. Don't take anything you read as gospel. Research it yourself. New research may show that some of this information is incorrect.

Also, *never stop taking any prescription medication without consulting your doctor.* Before you decide to undertake any dietary modification, lifestyle alteration, or a change in your medication, consult your doctor first, and let him or her know exactly what you intend to do.

MEASURING BLOOD PRESSURE

In his excellent book *Aging Myths*, physician Sigfried Kra points out that to get an accurate measure of your blood pressure, it's important to measure it in both arms, and to take readings while sitting and while standing.

Particularly in older people, atherosclerosis may involve the arteries of only one arm. If the blood flow is impaired in one arm, the affected arm will show a lower blood pressure reading, while the blood pressure in the other arm may be high. If both arms are not measured, the high blood pressure may go undetected.

Blood pressure is measured by getting two numbers called *systolic* and *diastolic* levels.

Diastolic pressure

Diastolic blood pressure is the pressure in your blood vessels when your heart is not pumping. Diastolic blood pressure less than 85 is considered normal. From 85 to 89 is considered *high normal*. From 90 to 104 is called *mild high blood pressure*, and over 105 is referred to as *moderate high blood pressure*. **If your diastolic pressure is 115 or higher, you have severe high blood pressure and are in some medical danger.**

Systolic pressure

Systolic blood pressure is the high point of your blood pressure, and occurs when your heart is pumping. Systolic pressure less than 140 is normal. Pressure from 140 to 150 is called *border-line systolic* high blood pressure. Systolic pressure of 160 or higher is known as *isolated systolic hypertension.* This last type of high blood pressure is often found in elderly people, where the diastolic pressure is normal.

What levels are considered high blood pressure?

You are considered to have high blood pressure if your diastolic blood pressure is 90 or over and your systolic blood pressure is 140 or over.

THE DANGERS OF HYPERTENSION

The cardiovascular system consists of the heart and blood vessels. During an average lifetime, the heart pumps more than *60 million gallons* of blood through more than 60,000 miles of blood vessels! The blood is responsible for taking oxygen and nutrients to every single cell in the body.

To understand what high blood pressure is, think of water running through a hose. The more water that runs through the hose, the higher the water pressure is going to be. If you squeeze the hose down so that the opening is smaller, the pressure gets higher. Blood vessels act just like a hose, and blockage or constriction of the blood vessels is what causes high blood pressure.

Constant high blood pressure is a *medical emergency*. It can damage blood vessels along with the organs that they feed. In extreme cases, blood vessels may even rupture. As we discussed previously, a blood vessel that ruptures in the brain causes a stroke.

High blood pressure is dangerous for several reasons. First, it's a leading contributor to *atherosclerosis* or cardiovascular disease, sometimes called hardening of the arteries. High blood pressure puts strain on the arteries and causes tiny breaks in the artery lining. This causes them to become scarred, stiff and hard. When this happens, small deposits of fat called *plaque* build up in the arteries, blocking them.

A healthy artery is as pliable and flexible as a rubber hose, but hypertension can damage an artery to the degree that it becomes as stiff as a piece of dry spaghetti. Arteries that become hardened and blocked are one of the major causes of strokes.

Fatty blockages and plaque in arteries, along with fluid buildup due to sodium retention or mineral imbalances, further elevate blood pressure. This makes the heart work harder and harder to pump the blood, and can eventually lead to heart failure or heart attack.

People over age 45 with high blood pressure are *three times* as likely to have a heart attack than those with normal

blood pressure, and are *five times* as likely to have a stroke than those with normal blood pressure.

High blood pressure is the foremost cause of stroke, and is one of the major causes of death among the elderly. The higher a person's blood pressure, the more likely it is that they will have a stroke. Even though women are less likely to have heart attacks then men, when it comes to strokes, women are just as vulnerable.

High blood pressure causes increased pressure in the internal organs and can promote damage to your kidneys, liver, and brain. Injury to the internal organs from high blood pressure happens silently, slowly, and without symptoms. But once it leads to a serious condition, the symptoms become very apparent.

People with high blood pressure have life spans on the average of 10 to 20 years shorter than people with normal blood pressure.

At the present time, no one knows for sure why people develop high blood pressure, but we do know that high blood pressure is one of the most treatable and preventable disorders.

TREATMENT FOR HIGH BLOOD PRESSURE

Because hypertension is the major contributor to cardiovascular related deaths, doctors have for years looked for ways to effectively lower blood pressure.

People with severe high blood pressure must take antihypertensive drugs. In such cases, the benefits of the drugs far outweigh the side effects. However, people with mild hypertension have the option of trying non-drug therapies.

Even though it's been shown clearly that dietary modification alone is often just as effective as many hypertensive medications, the majority of hypertensive patients are given prescription drugs to lower blood pressure without being offered any alternatives.

Unfortunately these drugs sometimes cause more problems than they cure. For example, several studies have shown that taking medication designed to lower blood pressure can actually increase the risk of having a heart attack.

In addition, many people fail to control their blood pressure with medication because they forget to take it. Because high blood pressure has no symptoms, people don't notice that they have skipped taking their medicine. Others stop taking the medicine because they don't like the side effects.

The drugs that are particularly toxic are the diuretics and the beta-blockers.

BETA-BLOCKERS

Beta-blocking drugs, such as propranolol (marketed under the brand name *Inderal*), are some of the most widely prescribed drugs in the United States today.

Beta-blockers lower blood pressure by decreasing the heart rate and the cardiac output. These drugs have many side effects, the most serious of which is congestive heart failure. Other common side effects include light-headedness, depression, memory loss, fatigue and sexual impotence.

It's also known that beta-blockers can trigger a rise in the level of cholesterol and triglycerides in the blood. This effect may explain why patients on beta-blockers have a higher incidence of heart attacks than high-risk patients not taking any medication.

It's been known for some time that several types of high blood pressure medication impair memory and intellectual capacity. Beta-blockers, such as propranolol and atenolol, may decrease memory performance more consistently than other antihypertensive agents that act through other mechanisms.

DIURETICS

As mentioned above, the other major class of hypertension drugs are the diuretics. These medications have also been shown to increase the risk of heart attack.

Diuretics work by eliminating water from the body, but they also increase the excretion of calcium, magnesium and potassium. These minerals actually lower blood pressure and prevent heart attacks. In addition, diuretics sometimes raise cholesterol levels.

Diuretics lower blood pressure by removing water from the cells of the body and passing it out of the body through urination. Kidneys monitor blood chemistry and make sure that the balance of water, waste products, and electrolytes is precisely maintained. But diuretics override this system.

Diuretics are used for a specific purpose—to get water out of the body. The result of the lower water level is reduced fluid tension in the blood vessels. But, unfortunately, fluid tension in *every cell* in the body is reduced.

Diuretics cause brain cells to excrete water, which under normal conditions, happens only in an extreme emergency. This loss of fluid causes people to feel dizzy and drowsy, and to have memory problems.

In most cases, these problems are bothersome but not serious. However, in older people, who already have less water in their tissues, further water excretion can cause brain function to be thrown off. For example, if an elderly person drinks alcohol, even in moderation, they can become so confused that they forget to consume enough water or to eat properly. This then leads to malnutrition and dehydration. In fact, **some doctors believe that the dehydration induced by diuretics combined with alcohol or tranquilizers is the leading cause of death among older Americans.**

While all of the above mentioned problems are called *side effects* of diuretics, they are not side effects at all, they are the main effect of the drug. A diuretic works by grabbing onto sodium atoms and causing the body to excrete extra salt. This in turn brings down the water level in all tissues, since water is bonded with the salt in the body.

Because potassium is close to sodium in its atomic structure, diuretics also cause the body to excrete potassium. Loss of potassium can lead to weakness, fatigue, and leg cramps.

Besides these common signs of potassium deficiency, there can be other complications. For example, *digitalis,* a drug given to heart patients to relieve their chest pain, becomes more toxic if the body is low in potassium.

There is some evidence that potassium deficiency is linked to high blood pressure, which means that a diuretic may actually be promoting the very condition that it's meant to cure.

All people taking diuretics should take a potassium supplement. Eating a diet high in potassium is not enough. It would take a truckload of bananas to replace the potassium lost from taking diuretics.

SEEKING NON-DRUG ALTERNATIVES

The irony behind these sometimes dangerous medical treatments is that non-drug therapies are supported by most medical authorities, especially for mild and moderate hypertension.

There have been numerous studies that show that the harmful side effects of beta-blockers and diuretics outweigh their therapeutic effects. These studies support the fact that effective lifestyle changes work as well as taking drugs.

Many doctors, including those on the Joint National Committee on Detection, Evaluation and Treatment of High Blood Pressure, recommend that most people with high blood pressure not be placed on drugs, but instead say these patients should be encouraged to make dietary and lifestyle changes.

FACTORS THAT RAISE BLOOD PRESSURE

FOOD ALLERGY

Several studies have shown that blood pressure can be raised by food allergies. If you have a history of allergies or if there is a history of allergies in your family, it may be worthwhile to engage in an elimination and allergic rotation diet to find out if it can lower your blood pressure. Several studies have shown a positive relation between food allergies and a rise in blood pressure. For information on elimination and rotation diets, consult an allergist. More information on allergies can be found in the book *Brain Allergies,* by W.H. Philpott, M.D., and D.W. Kalita, Ph.D.

SUGAR

In one experiment, the blood pressure of twenty healthy men was examined after they consumed various sugar solutions following an over-night fast. *Drinking* sugar raised their blood pressure for two hours. *Eating* sugar produced a significant increase in blood pressure that lasted for an hour. In light of these results, it may be a good idea to minimize your sugar intake.

ALCOHOL

Medical evidence shows that drinking more than three beers a day, more than three glasses of wine daily or three mixed drinks in a 24 hour period raises blood pressure.

DRUGS THAT RAISE BLOOD PRESSURE
Alcohol
Oral contraceptives
Decongestant nose drops
Anti-inflammatory drugs
Estrogen
Steroids
Medicine containing sodium
Ibuprofin

However, drinking moderately can be good for you. There is some data that suggest drinking a glass of red wine a day can actually lower moderately high blood pressure. Keep in mind that alcoholic beverages are very high in calories, so if you are trying to lose weight, alcohol is not going to help.

SMOKING

If you're a smoker, quit. This is absolutely essential. Smoking drastically increases your risk of dying of cardiovascular disease. Smoking also causes an immediate temporary increase in blood pressure during the time a person is smoking the cigarette. But because of its negative effect on the cardiovascular system, the long-term effect of smoking may be permanent hypertension.

LICORICE

Although most licorice flavored products in this country contain artificial flavor, real licorice contains a substance called *gly-*

cyrrhizic acid which can increase blood pressure.

This substance causes the body to retain sodium and excrete potassium. In addition, licorice can increase the side effects of diuretics. Real licorice is found today in some laxatives, natural licorice candy, some tobacco products, and in many natural cough remedies. Check labels before using these products.

LEAD

Lead levels that were previously considered safe are now found to be associated with increased blood pressure. Eliminate all sources of lead and cadmium in your diet and, if necessary, get chelation therapy. (For more about lead, see Chapter 18, Neurotoxins and Memory.)

CADMIUM

People with hypertension show blood cadmium levels three or four times higher than those in matched people with normal blood pressure. Cadmium is found in high levels in cigarettes. It's been found that taking zinc supplements counteracts the effect of cadmium toxicity that raises blood pressure. This does *not* offset the other negative effects of smoking, however.

SALT

The average American consumes about two to two and a half teaspoons of salt a day. That's more than twenty times the amount of salt the body actually needs. In Japan, citizens consume enormous amounts of salt, perhaps the highest in the world. *Jane Brody's Nutrition Book* states that stroke caused by high blood pressure is the number one cause of death in Japan. And it's been found that 40% of the people in Japan have high blood pressure.

Conversely, in New Guinea, in the Amazon areas, and in the highlands of Malaysia, where people eat very little salt in their diet, there is no hypertension.

When you eat something salty, you get thirsty because extra water is needed to dilute the salt. The extra salt causes the body to hold water, and causes the volume of blood to rise. Blood vessels become water-logged, and they then become more sensitive to nerve stimulation, which cause them to contract. As more blood has to go through the contracted smaller vessels, blood pressure increases.

Even though salt usually raises blood pressure, it affects some people differently. Over half of the people with high blood pressure are *salt sensitive*. Adding salt to their diet makes blood pressure go up significantly. Salt sensitivity is found more commonly among blacks, individuals that are overweight, and those that have a genetic family history of high blood pressure. If you fall within one of these categories, salt should be avoided completely.

Other people with high blood pressure are *salt resistant*. Their blood pressure does not change when they vary the amount of salt they eat.

There are a small amount of people who are *reverse salt sensitive*. These people's blood pressure increases when they reduce salt.

If you decide you must eliminate salt from your diet, remove the salt shaker from your table. Cut out foods like ham, bacon, hot dogs, shell fish, cheeses, avocado and all processed foods. Also avoid antacids and laxatives that are high in sodium. Become aware of the hidden salt in fast food and prepared foods. Read labels very carefully.

You can lower the salt content in prepared food and canned goods by simply rinsing them in water. For example, in one study, the salt in a can of tuna rinsed in water for one minute was reduced by 79%.

TALKING

Strange as it may seem, it has been found that talking causes a temporary increase in blood pressure. In fact, some people with normal blood pressure have been diagnosed in the doctor's office as having hypertension merely because they were talking while their blood pressure was being measured.

SNORING

Sleep studies show that snoring raises blood pressure. Sleep apnea, a disorder that blocks the flow of air through the eso- phagus temporarily, can rapidly raise blood pressure, and can be potentially dangerous.

Men who snore frequently actually have a 50% higher risk of having high blood pressure, a 70% increased potential for heart disease, and a 40% higher risk of stroke. Women who snore are 30% more likely to have elevated blood pressure.

This condition also causes sleep deprivation and constant fatigue, because the person wakes up each time the airway becomes blocked.

There are now several simple non-medical and surgical techniques that can eliminate this problem. If you are a chronic snorer, see a specialist who can offer you several remedies for the problem.

For more information, write to the American Sleep Apnea Association, 2025 Pennsylvania Avenue NW, Suite 905, Washington, DC 20006, telephone (202) 293-3650.

NUTRITIONAL FACTORS IN LOWERING BLOOD PRESSURE

WATER

Some research suggests that increasing the amount of water that you drink can lower blood pressure. Dr. F. Batmanghelidj, in his book, *Your Body's Many Cries for Water*, feels that dehydration is a major cause of high blood pressure, and that increased fluid intake is the cure.

He also recommends that you avoid all foods that contain caffeine, such as coffee, tea and soft drinks, because caffeine has diuretic properties. He suggests that every person should drink six to eight glasses of water per day.

WEIGHT REDUCTION

It is clear that one of the most powerful contributors to high blood pressure is excess weight. This is evidenced by the fact that 70% of people with hypertension are overweight.

High blood pressure is more common in overweight people than in those of normal weight because every extra pound of body fat requires an additional mile of blood vessels to feed the cells. This extra mileage forces the heart to work harder.

The good news is that weight-induced high blood pressure can be reduced dramatically through weight loss alone. Several studies suggest that overweight people can decrease their blood pressure eight to ten points just by losing twenty pounds.

The most effective way to lose weight and consequently lower your blood pressure is to permanently increase your physical activity and eliminate all fat from your diet.

LOW-FAT DIET

Eating a low-fat diet reduces blood pressure, even if body weight remains the same. In one particularly interesting study, thirty five healthy, middle-aged men and women changed their diet from one which nearly 40% of calories were from fat to a regimen that included only 20% fat.

After six weeks on the reduced fat diet, diastolic blood pressure was lowered by an average of nine points.

A diet high in fresh fruits and vegetables which includes only low-fat meats, such as chicken, turkey and fish, lowers fat intake dramatically.

VEGETARIANISM

People who eat vegetarian diets have significantly cleaner arteries and lower blood pressure than meat eaters. Doctor Ross Trattler in his book, *Better Health Through Natural Healing*, states, "Over 85% of the people with high blood pressure can be treated without drugs. In most cases, dietary modification is all that is needed." He recommends the most effective way to treat high blood pressure is a vegetarian diet.

Melvin Werbach has spent years researching the nutritional influences on illness. Werbach recommends above all, an increase in fiber intake. He cites various studies that show that fiber decreases blood pressure. Like Trattler, Werbach suggests that the best way to achieve this is through a vegetarian diet.

RAW FOODS

Studies show that people who increase the amount of raw foods in their diet can actually lower their blood pressure significantly.

Various Cuts of Chicken and Turkey and Their Fat Content
(3 ounces for each except thigh as noted)

1/2 Chicken Breast without Skin	4.0 grams
1 2-oz. Chicken Thigh without Skin	5.7 grams
1 Chicken Leg w/ Thigh and No Skin	8.0 grams
4 Chicken Wings	6.8 grams
Turkey White Meat	2.7 grams
Turkey Dark Meat	6.1 grams

A Dozen Types of Fish and Their Fat Content
(3 ounces for each)

Cod, Atlantic, cooked	7.0 grams
Flounder, cooked	11.7 grams
Haddock, cooked	7.5 grams
Halibut, cooked	18.9 grams
Mackerel, Pacific, raw	28.8 grams
Monkfish, raw	18.0 grams
Orange Roughy, raw	50.4 grams
Salmon, Atlantic, raw	40.1 grams
Sardines, Atlantic, canned in oil	50.4 grams
Sea Bass, cooked	18.8 grams
Shark, raw	30.8 grams
Trout, Lake, raw	40.0 grams

In addition, several studies have revealed that increasing the amount of raw food in the diet resulted in weight loss and a spontaneous decrease in the consumption of nicotine and alcohol. It seems that the improvement in nutritional status of the body reduces the craving for these substances.

FRUIT

In his book *How to Develop a Sky High I.Q.*, Jeffery Bland states that certain tropical fruits clean out arteries. These include bananas, kiwi, mangoes and papaya. An enzyme in these fruits, called *bromelin*, is responsible for this effect.

Grapefruit and apple pectin lower cholesterol and keep arteries clean. In one research study, people who consumed twelve grams of grapefruit pectin a day lowered their cholesterol by 17%. Grapefruit pectin capsules are available in health food stores.

Eating fruit is important. For example, it's been shown that just eating one serving of fruit per day can lower stroke risk by as much as 40%.

OLIVE OIL

Certain types of fats, called *polyunsaturated* and *monounsaturated* fats, are found in fish, vegetable oils, seeds and nuts. These fats lower blood pressure and neutralize the negative effects of saturated fats. The most highly unsaturated or mono-unsaturated fats available are olive oil and canola oil. One teaspoon of olive oil per 1,000 calories of intake reduces blood pressure as much as 10 points.

FISH OILS

Ocean fish are high in a substance called MAX epa, which is one of the omega three fatty acids. Omega-3 has been shown to lower blood pressure. Fish high in omega-3 fatty acids include mackerel, sardines, salmon and haddock. (Of course, you'll want to combine any high-fat content fish with low-fat food items for a healthier diet.) You can also buy omega-3 fatty acids in concentrated form in your health food store.

It appears that fish oils lower blood pressure by decreasing the viscosity of the blood and making it flow more smoothly through the blood vessel. When fish oil is eaten, it is immediately taken up by blood platelets and red blood cells. The oils reduce the tendency of the platelets to stick together, which prevents clots. The presence of the oils in red cells makes the cells more flexible, and the increased flexibility makes them more slippery.

FIBER

Eating a diet high in plant fiber can lower blood pressure, although the mechanism is not clearly understood. Some studies show that by tripling the amount of fiber in the diet, people have reduced their systolic blood pressure by as much as 11%.

It's thought that increased fiber has this effect because it regulates changes in insulin levels. There is some evidence that high levels of insulin contribute to high blood pressure because it's a salt retentive hormone. High fiber foods include all vegetables and fresh fruits and whole grains.

NUTRITIONAL STATUS

Studies show nutritional differences between people with normal blood pressure and high blood pressure. People with high blood pressure tend to have lower levels of vitamin A, lower vitamin B complex, vitamin C and vitamin D. This suggests that supplementing all of these vitamins would lower blood pressure.

COENZYME Q$_{10}$

Another nutrient that's been shown to be deficient in high blood pressure patients is coenzyme Q$_{10}$. The recommended daily allowance for lowering of blood pressure with coenzyme Q$_{10}$ is 60mg. per day. It is said to take four to twelve weeks for this nutrient to lower blood pressure.

POTASSIUM

As mentioned previously, diuretics leach potassium from the body. Anyone taking diuretics should also take a potassium supplement.

Supplementing your diet with potassium can reduce blood pressure. Studies show that potassium supplements have little effect on people with normal blood pressure, but they do reduce blood pressure in people with high blood pressure. Winter squash, cantaloupe, avocados, orange juice, bananas, potatoes, and tomatoes are all high in potassium.

Julian Whitaker, in *99 Secrets for a Longer Healthier Life,* says the following about blood pressure: "It's not just the amount of salt that we take in every day that causes high blood pressure, but it's the ratio of sodium to potassium. In our culture, potassium is reduced in our diet by food processing and sodium is added to our diet by food processing. By increasing your potassium intake, you can lower your blood pressure without reducing sodium."

Here are several ideas for increasing your potassium intake. You can use one or more of these suggestions each day.

•   Drink an 8-ounce glass of orange juice daily.

•   Eat a salad of uncooked, fresh vegetables every day.

•   Eat two apples a day.

•   Use a potassium-based salt substitute.

If you have a kidney problem, check with your doctor before attempting to increase the potassium you take in. Potassium salt substitutes are found in grocery stores under the names *Morton's Salt Substitute, Nu-Salt* and *No Salt.*

CALCIUM

Calcium is found in dairy products, all of the bean family, and in leafy green vegetables.

It's been determined that people with high blood pressure consume less calcium than people with normal blood pressure. In a study at the University of Oregon, hypertensives were given 1,000mg of calcium a day. At the end of eight weeks, twenty one of them had reduced their blood pressure by ten points or better.

Calcium helps lower high blood pressure by aiding in the excretion of excess sodium, it also relaxes the blood vessels.

MAGNESIUM

Magnesium is another important nutrient to lowering blood pressure. Magnesium is found in nuts, brown rice, milk, wheat germ, bananas, potatoes, molasses and soy products. Low levels of magnesium in the diet have been shown to increase blood pressure. Magnesium acts in concert with calcium in regulating blood pressure.

Some new drugs on the market are called *calcium channel blockers*. These drugs work by altering the access of calcium into the cell. These medications relax smooth muscle in the artery wall and cause a patient's blood pressure to fall. Taking magnesium causes the same type of thing to happen, with none of the side effects. It might be called a natural calcium channel blocker.

Taking 1,000mg of magnesium every day has been shown to relax blood vessels and reduce peripheral resistance.

It's thought that one of the reasons magnesium lowers blood pressure is because this compound is a vasodilator. This means that it can widen the diameter of a blood vessel. Magnesium is able to accomplish this task by removing calcium from the smooth muscle cell surfaces inside the blood vessels.

Dr. Julian Whitaker has a specific approach to treatment for severe cases of hypertension. He uses injections of 2 grams of magnesium sulfate mixed with procaine. In addition, he recommends a very rigid diet, consisting only of brown rice, raw fruit, and raw and cooked vegetables. Whitaker claims that even severe cases of high blood pressure can be brought substantially under control on this strict diet along with the magnesium injections. This is a radical program, so never attempt it without a doctor's supervision.

RICE

In his book, *The Nature Doctor,* Dr. H. Vogel states that eating daily servings of whole grain rice can reduce blood pressure. Rice is a low-fat, high-fiber food that also promotes weight loss, and even if Vogel is wrong, rice is good for you.

COLEUS

A member of the mint family, Coleus grows in India. It's cultivated in the United States as an ornamental plant. The root has been used for medicinal purposes and as a condiment for salads.

Coleus has been used for hundreds of years in Hindu and Ayurvedic traditional medicine because it's the source of a unique compound called *forskolin.*

Forskolin has been shown to have an anti-spasmodic affect on smooth muscles, which are the type of muscles found in the walls of the blood vessels. Using coleus lowers blood pressure, and improves the contraction of the heart muscle. This chemical has also been shown to be effective in treatment of glaucoma, and has the ability to prevent asthma attacks in some people.

HAWTHORNE

Hawthorne leaves, berries and blossoms contain many bio-logically active compounds called *flavonoids*. These compounds are responsible for the red and blue color of berries, and also cause the red and blue color of cherries, grapes and many flowers. Flavonoids are highly concentrated in hawthorne berries.

Hawthorne extracts are effective in lowering blood pressure, reducing angina attacks, lowering serum cholesterol levels, and preventing the deposit of cholesterol in the arterial walls. Hawthorne is widely used in Europe and Asia for its anti-hypertensive activity.

Hawthorne appears to improve the blood supply to the heart by dilating the coronary arteries. It improves the metabolic processes of the heart, which results in an increase in the force of contractions of the heart muscle, and eliminates some types of rhythm disturbances by inhibiting an enzyme in the body called *angiotensin converting enzyme* (ACE). Hawthorne's ability to dilate coronary arteries has been repeatedly dem-onstrated in experimental studies. This effect appears to come from the relaxation of smooth muscle in the blood vessels.

Recently, several substances in hawthorne have been shown to inhibit ACE in a similar way to *catapril,* a drug that is used to treat high blood pressure.

In order for hawthorne to work effectively, it must be taken at least two weeks before adequate tissue concentrations are achieved. The dosage of hawthorne depends on the type of preparation and the source of the material. Check with a qualified herbalist for proper dosage.

GUGULIPID

Gugulipid is a remarkable compound that lowers cholesterol. Also called Gugul, this substance is an extract of the *mukomur* tree, a traditional Indian medicinal plant. Gugul is an effective lipid-lowering agent, which means it decreases both cholesterol and triglyceride levels.

Gugul is extremely effective because it brings down LDL cholesterol while elevating HDL. Studies show that gugul prevents atherosclerosis and aids in the regression of pre-existing atherosclerotic plaques.

Gugulipid appears to prevent heart damage from free radicals, and also improves the metabolism of the heart. It also mildly inhibits platelets from clumping together in blood vessels.

In addition it's been shown that gugul has an ability to stimulate the thyroid function. This thyroid-stimulating effect may, in fact, be responsible for some of Gugulipid's fat-lowering ability.

GARLIC

The *Journal of Longevity Research* recommends garlic as an effective treatment for high blood pressure. Although many doctors debate the usefulness of garlic, several studies show that the regular use of garlic supplements can lower blood pressure. It appears that the benefits are temporary, and the supplements must be used continuously to be of benefit.

CELERY

Celery has been used as a folk remedy for lowering blood pressure for many generations. Although celery contains large amounts of sodium, it also appears to contain substances which lower blood pressure. Nutritionist recommend eating two stalks of celery every day.

ALFALFA

Alfalfa contains a chemical called *fibosterol*, which is a naturally occurring plant substance that neutralizes harmful cholesterol.

BLACK COHOSH

This herb is recommended by many herbalists as having positive effects on high blood pressure, but I was unable to find any scientific studies to verify this.

CAYENNE PEPPER

Cayenne has been shown to reduce cholesterol and blood pressure. It is available in capsule form in health food stores. Contrary to what many believe, for the majority of us, cayenne pepper does not irritate the stomach.

APPLE CIDER VINEGAR

Apple cider vinegar and honey is a well-known folk remedy for high blood pressure. The best way to take it is by diluting two tablespoons of vinegar into a glass of water and sip it during a meal. You can add honey to improve the taste. You can also add vinegar to the diet in salad dressings and in cooking. This remedy is said to reduce blood pressure up to 20%.

VALERIAN ROOT

Valerian root causes a tranquilizing effect on the brain and the nervous system. It is an important herb for lowering stress, which is a cause of high blood pressure.

CHERVIL

Chervil is an herb that has been used for years to lower blood pressure, although I could find no scientific studies that prove it is effective. The leaves and flowers are the parts of the plant that are utilized for this purpose.

CHIVES

Chives are a member of the onion family, and like garlic, can help lower blood pressure. They contain the sulfur-rich oil found in garlic, but in smaller quantities. It is best to use chives along with other herbs for this purpose.

SERPENTWOOD

Serpentwood is an herb that has been used for many years to lower blood pressure. It has been used in India for over four thousand years.

HYPERBALANCE

Vita Industries manufactures a natural blood pressure lowering product which is a mixture of roots and herbs. Called *Hyper-*

balance, the product includes garlic, dandelion root, and several vitamins. I have no information on the effectiveness of this product.

OTHER METHODS OF LOWERING BLOOD PRESSURE

EXERCISE

The first and most important non-drug therapy for high blood pressure is exercise. Exercise can be a very effective treatment for moderately high blood pressure, but it takes time to see the effects. In some cases it takes almost up to a year, but most people see results within three months.

To reduce blood pressure effectively, the exercise must be *aerobic,* that is, it must be exercise that raises the pulse to your target heart rate for at least a half an hour. To establish your target heart rate, subtract your age from 220, and multiply the result by 85%.

Aerobic exercise doesn't have to be grueling. A brisk walk for 30 or 40 minutes, three or four times a week, is effective. At that rate, it will take four to six months to lower blood pressure.

Although aerobic exercise is very good for lowering blood pressure, isometric exercises like weight lifting, are not good. Weight lifting can actually cause blood pressure to sky-rocket. If you have high blood pressure, talk to your doctor before beginning a weight lifting program.

STRESS REDUCTION

Years of research have shown that stress reduction training such as meditation, self-hypnosis and breathing techniques, can lower the tension in the body, and also lower blood pressure.

Exercise also lowers stress and tension in the body and therefore has a doubly good effect. If you think that stress may be causing your high blood pressure, one of the ways to find out is to take your blood pressure several times a day during different situations. Identify any pattern in your blood pressure related to stress. For example, if you take your blood pressure right after a stressful situation, is it significantly higher? If so, begin a stress reduction program.

Although most stress reduction seminars focus primarily on relaxation methods, the most effective method of stress management is *coping skills*, that is, learning effective communication skills and effective problem-solving skills. Gaining these skills makes life considerably easier.

PETS

Getting a pet can significantly lower blood pressure. While pets are very effective for this, it has been shown that even taking care of plants can lower blood pressure. Living with plants or pets involves bonding, commitment, and emotional gratification, which in turn reduce stress.

In one study, 92 people who had suffered a heart attack were discharged from a coronary care unit in the hospital, and monitored frequently. Thirty-nine of them owned pets, and fifty three did not. One year later, the mortality rate of the people with no pets was 28%,while the mortality rate of the people with pets was only 6%! Get a pet.

HUMAN TOUCH

It has also been found that physical touch lowers blood pressure. Caressing, holding, loving, massaging and stroking, significantly lowers blood pressure in people. So, if you can't get a pet, get a mate.

SOCIAL SUPPORT

It's very clear from scientific research that people with many friends and a large social support network have less stress in their life, less problems, and lower blood pressure than people who don't have the support.

HAPPINESS

It's also been shown that people who are happy have lower blood pressure than people that are worried and anxious. This is hard evidence that you should put some fun in your life.

Research has also shown the longer that people live together, the more likely it is that their blood pressure will become the same. This suggests that if your blood pressure is high, there is a good chance that your spouse's blood pressure is high also. Monitor your blood pressure together. Apparently happy people have a positive effect on each other, while unhappy people have a negative effect.

CHAPTER FOURTEEN

A WHACK ON THE HEAD

Magnum enters the darkened room with his gun drawn. He knows that there are two armed men in the room, and his next move could be his last.

As he inches around a packing crate, a sinister figure appears above him. Suddenly without warning, the villain hits him with the butt of his gun, knocking him unconscious. Magnum falls to the floor in a heap.

Several minutes later, he awakens to find himself a prisoner. Slowly coming back to consciousness, he unexpectedly jumps up, tackles the villain, and overpowers him.

We've all watched scenes like this hundreds of times on television. Villains and heroes alike are constantly getting smacked on the head with guns, and are knocked out by a punch in the nose. They recover within minutes and go on about their business with no ill effects.

But things don't happen that way in the real world. A blow to the head that causes a loss of consciousness can inflict one of several types of serious injury.

Being knocked unconscious can cause a *closed head injury*. This condition is caused by the bruising or tearing of delicate brain tissue. The brain is a jelly-like substance that is suspended in a bath of spinal fluid. It is protected by rubbery membranes called the *meninges*. Minor bumps on the head do not usually cause any damage. But getting hit hard enough to cause a loss of consciousness can cause serious injury to the brain's delicate tissues.

A *concussion* is a temporary loss of consciousness occurring after a blow to the head. The impact of the blow causes the semi-liquid brain tissue to slosh about inside the skull, causing it to bruise. Like any bruise, the injured tissue then swells. When the brain becomes bruised and swollen, brain function can be disrupted for weeks after the injury. This can cause loss of memory, and sometimes permanent brain damage.

Most concussions are caused by traffic accidents, but they can also occur from falls, or from being hit on the head by any object.

Immediately after a concussion, the victim may experience confusion, memory loss, vomiting, and blurred vision. The longer the person is unconscious, the more severe the symptoms tend to be.

As soon as possible after a person has experienced a loss of consciousness, she should see a doctor to rule out skull fracture, brain injury, or bleeding inside the lining of the brain called *subdural hematoma*. Subdural bleeding is a serious condition that requires immediate medical attention.

Weeks after a head injury, the person may experience headaches, dizziness, changes in behavior, drowsiness, and memory loss.

About one-third of the people who experience a concussion will exhibit *post concussion syndrome*. This syndrome includes chronic memory loss, dizziness, and changes in behavior that can last over a year. Because most knocks on the head are soon forgotten, the person usually does not connect the symptoms with the accident.

Repeated concussions, such as those experienced by boxers, can cause permanent brain damage, including a condition called *punch drunk syndrome.* One study revealed that 87% of former boxers showed evidence of brain damage. We also know that a significant number of those suffering from dementia have a history of head injury.

Elderly people often fall or bump their head, and later forget that the incident happened. In a younger person, these bumps may be unimportant. But the brains of elderly people are sometimes smaller, and slosh about inside the skull more easily. The decreased amount of neurons in the elderly brain makes minor damage more serious. Even minor bumps on the head in the elderly, such as a bump on the head from a cabinet door, can cause subdural hematoma. So any bump on the head should be checked out by a doctor.

CHAPTER FIFTEEN

DEPRESSION AND MEMORY

Depression is the most common mental disorder in our nation. In fact, one out of two hospital beds in this country is occupied by someone suffering from depression. What is less recognized is the fact that depression is also one of the most frequent and under-diagnosed causes of memory problems.

Each year, hundreds of people seek help from physicians and psychologists for memory problems, when what they are actually suffering from is depression.

Depression has a profound effect on the ability to think, reason and remember. In fact, the symptoms of depression can be so severe that it's often difficult to tell whether a person is suffering from depression or dementia. Because of this, several diagnostic tests have been developed to ferret out the differences between these two memory destroying disorders.

If you feel that you have a serious memory problem, you should have a neuropsychological examination to discover if your problem is, in fact, depression. This is very important because untreated depression increases the level of a group of chemicals called *glucocorticoids*. These chemicals cause permanent damage to the hippocampus, the part of the brain that stores memory.

HOW DEPRESSION EFFECTS MEMORY

Depression interferes with memory in several ways.

First, depressed people become focused on internal events. These may be memories about tragic losses, or about real and imagined transgressions. Often the focus is on physical symptoms such as body aches and pains. This internal preoccupation prevents the person from attending to the outside world and interferes with memory storage.

Second, depression actually slows down the level of brain activity in the afflicted person, so that memory and thought processing are impaired. People suffering from depression often are said to exhibit *poverty of thought,* which is the inability to process thought at all.

Third, depression is accompanied by feelings of helplessness and hopelessness. This leads the sufferer to ignore any input from the outside world. They just don't care if they remember anything.

Fourth, depression has also been linked to decreased levels of chemicals in the brain, called *neurotransmitters.* The neurotransmitters involved in depression include *serotonin, melatonin, dopamine, adrenaline,* and *noradrenaline,* substances which also play an important role in memory. It is believed that antidepressant drugs work by raising the levels of these chemicals.

CAUSES OF DEPRESSION

Although depression is most often caused by loss and isolation or a biochemical imbalance in the brain, it can also be triggered by nutritional deficiencies or excesses, prescription, over-the-counter and illegal drugs; alcohol, caffeine and nicotine; hypoglycemia; aspartame (Nutrasweet); and hormonal imbalances.

In fact, research suggests that almost any chronic nutritional deficiency or imbalance can cause depression.

Several medications, especially blood pressure medications, can cause depression and subsequent memory problems. Even though this is common knowledge, many doctors are unaware of how often people suffer from drug-induced depression.

Harvard researcher Dr. Jerry Avorn and his colleagues looked at how often antidepressants were prescribed to people taking beta-blockers such as Inderal, Lopressor, and Corgard.

Examining the medical records of 143,253 patients, they found that 23% (almost one out of four) of those taking beta-blockers were also taking antidepressants.

This study also revealed that doctors often give patients additional prescriptions to overcome side effects of another medication without realizing that the problems could be solved by eliminating the first medication. For this reason, ask your doctor if any medication you are taking might cause depression.

In addition to medication problems, depression can also be brought on by allergies and environmental toxins. For example, solvents like those used in paints, furniture making, and boat building have been reported to evoke depression, confusion, and memory loss in many people. Another cause is chronic exposure to heavy metals. When this is a suspected source of the problem, hair analysis is an accurate and cost effective method of detecting heavy metals, and should be used to aid the diagnosis.

Depression is often one of the first signs of thyroid disease. Even subtle decreases in thyroid hormone can induce depression. For this reason, depressed patients should be routinely screened for hyperthyroidism, particularly if they complain of fatigue. Like the thyroid gland, dysfunction of the

---

DRUGS THAT CAUSE
DEPRESSION

Digitalis	Cimetidine
Clonidine	Methyldopate
Levodopa	Barbiturates
Antipsychotics	Benzodiazepines
Propranolol	Steroids
Reserpine	Alcohol

---

adrenal gland has been associated with depression, so adrenal function should also be checked.

In a few cases, chronic vitamin C deficiency has been shown to cause hypochondriasis and depression. In contrast, high levels of vitamin C seem to have a positive effect on multiple functions of the brain.

Folic acid and B_{12} levels are low in a large proportion of patients suffering from various emotional problems, especially depression. But although B_{12} deficiency is common in depression, measuring levels of B_{12} in the blood is not useful. B_{12} deficiency may not become apparent until long after serum levels have been greatly reduced, and depression has begun.

Folic acid deficiency is the most common nutritional deficiency in the world. In studies of people with depression, as many as 30% were shown to be deficient in folic acid. This deficiency is especially prevalent in the elderly. In one study, 67% of the patients admitted to a geropsychiatric hospital were folate deficient. Folic acid deficiency can causes chronic forgetfulness, insomnia, apathy, depression, and dementia-like symptoms.

Niacin (vitamin B_3) deficiency and biotin deficiency can also bring on depression and memory problems, as well as cause emotional instability, while a pantothenic acid (vitamin B_5) and pyridoxine (vitamin B_6) deficiency can cause restlessness, irritability, and depression.

Thiamin (vitamin B_1) deficiency is very common among alcoholics, and can lead to a condition called Korsakoff's psychosis, which causes profound memory loss, as well as depression, apathy, anxiety and irritability. B_1 deficiency in the brain results in a condition called *metabolic acidosis*, which upsets the neurotransmitter balance.

PEA

Phenylalanine is an amino acid found in food. It is transformed in the body to a chemical called *phenylethylamine,* or PEA. PEA is also found in high concentrations in chocolate. This compound has amphetamine like properties.

Low urinary PEA levels are found in depressed patients, and because of this, it's been suggested that PEA is a natural antidepressant.

Taking supplements of the amino acid phenylalanine is said to increase PEA production. But direct phenylethylamine replacement is also effective against depression, and has been shown to have long-term effects in combating it.

Dr. Hector Sabelli at Rush University in Chicago reported that twelve out of fourteen patients successfully treated with PEA and *selegiline* (also known as deprenyl) remained free of symptoms for twenty to fifty weeks after treatment ceased. The patients continued to experience therapeutic benefits and reported no adverse side effects from the treatment. The results of this study suggest that lowered levels of PEA play a role in depression in a significant number of patients, and that PEA treatment works for relieving depressive symptoms.

SAM

A substance called *S-Adenosyl-methionine* (SAM) has been shown to be an effective antidepressant. Its effect is comparable to the tricyclic antidepressants, and several studies have proven it to be safe and effective. Improvement is usually noted within four to seven days, and no side effects have been reported.

BIOPTERIN

Recently a vitamin-like compound called *tetrahydro-biopterin* (also called biopterin and BH4) has been found to be a useful antidepressant. In the body, biopterin plays a crucial role in the manufacture of the numerous neurotransmitters mentioned above.

It's been found that patients with recurrent depressions have reduced tetrahydro-biopterin synthesis, and these patients respond well to supplementation of this substance. Although this chemical is not available yet in the United States, its production can be stimulated by taking folic acid, vitamin B_{12}, and Vitamin C. It's possible, therefore, to increase vitamin levels and stimulate BH4 formation.

OTHER TREATMENTS

Treatment of depression begins by eliminating possible environmental toxins and nutritional imbalances. Once this is done, cognitive therapy is very helpful. If therapy alone does not relieve the symptoms, antidepressant medication can be very effective. Effective treatment of depression is often all that's needed to correct long-standing memory problems. For more information about depression, contact the following organizations:

The National Foundation for Depressive Illness
PO Box 2257
New York, NY 10116.
(800) 248-4344.

The National Alliance for the Mentally Ill
200 North Glebe Road
Suite 1015
Arlington, VA 22203-3754
(800) 950-NAMI

The National Mental Health Association
1021 Prince St.
Alexandria, VA 22314
(800) 969-NMHA

The Obsessive Compulsive Foundation
PO Box 70
Milford, CT 06460
(203) 878-5669

The Anxiety Disorders Association of America
6000 Executive Blvd.
Suite 513
Rockville, MD 20852
(301) 231-9350

The National Depressive and Manic-Depressive Association
730 North Franklin St.
Suite 501
Chicago, IL 60610
(800) 826-3632

SYMPTOMS OF DEPRESSION

THINKING

Negative self-evaluations
Negative expectations
Negative interpretation of
events
Memory loss
Confusion
Impaired attention span
A focus on past mistakes
All or nothing thinking
Unwanted thoughts
Poverty of thought
Hopelessness
Helplessness
The wish to be dead
Suicidal thoughts
The conviction of being a
burden

EMOTIONS

Ambivalence
No sense of humor
Feeling inadequate
Chronic apathy
Sadness
Guilt
Powerlessness
Emotions are dulled
No motivation

SYMBOLIC

Destructive fantasies
Nightmares
Bothersome images
Punishment from God

BEHAVIOR

A change in activity level
Aggression
Destructive acts
Crying spells
Suicide attempts
Slowed speech
Substance abuse
Impulsiveness
Violation of personal values
Agitation
Perfectionism

RELATIONSHIPS

A "victim" relational style
Extreme dependency
High reactivity
Social isolation
Avoidance
Approval seeking
Martyrdom
Passive-aggressive behavior
Boundary problems
Hypercritical
Poor communication skills

PHYSICAL

Multiple physical complaints
Sleep problems
Appetite changes
Weight changes
Change in sex-drive

CHAPTER SIXTEEN
HORMONES AND MEMORY

Hormones are molecules that regulate the complex balance of the many systems in the body. They are secreted into the body through an intricate system of organs called *ductless glands*. Because hormones work in concert with one another, and they control the major metabolic functions, almost any hormonal imbalance has the potential to upset normal memory function.

THYROTOXICOSIS

Thyrotoxicosis is a syndrome that occurs as a result of excess thyroid hormone. This can result from the body manufacturing too much hormone, or when the hormone is taken as a medication. A person with this syndrome feels tense, excitable, and emotionally unstable. They may have temper tantrums, crying spells, and episodes of euphoria.

People with this syndrome have feelings of constant physical fatigue, but they also have a need to remain active. Impaired attention, concentration, and memory are common symptoms. Other common complaints include heart palpitations, shortness of breath, muscle weakness and insomnia. This condition is often confused with an anxiety disorder, especially in women.

HYPOTHYROIDISM

Hypothyroidism is caused by a lack of adequate thyroid hormone. Symptoms of this disorder include cold hands and feet, menstrual problems, dry skin, thinning hair, low energy, slowness of mental processes, slow speech, and impaired recent memory. Depression is also common. Dr.Broda Barnes in his book, *Hypothyroidism: the Unsuspected Illness*, lists forty-seven symptoms that he feels are related to low thyroid. According to Barnes, body temperature below 97.8 degrees is one indication of hypothyroidism.

The treatment for this condition is supplementing the body with synthetic thyroid hormone. This should only be done under careful supervision of a physician.

HYPOPARATHYROIDISM

The parathyroid gland is located in the neck. It regulates immune function. *Hypoparathyroidism* is a malfunction of this gland. Most people with this disorder are women over fifty who have been ill for a prolonged period of time.

More than half of the people with parathyroid problems develop psychiatric symptoms. The symptoms usually begin as irritability and a lack of initiative. The disorder then progresses into depression, marked by the loss of interest in eating, social withdrawal, and memory problems.

In one study of fifty four patients with hypoparathyroidism, thirty six had mood disorders, twelve had memory problems, and five had psychotic episodes. Thirty-seven percent of the patients showed personality changes. All of these problems disappeared when the disorder was treated.

Malfunction of the parathyroid causes *hypocalcemia,* a deficiency of calcium. Supplementing the diet with 1500 mg of calcium a day helps.

ADDISON'S DISEASE

Addison's disease is caused by a malfunction of the adrenal glands which leads to decreased levels of chemicals called *corticosteroids* (which include aldosterone, cortisol, and adrenal androgens). The mental symptoms caused by this problem include apathy, fatigue, lack of initiative, depression, and memory loss.

CORTISONE

Cortisone is an important hormone that regulates bio-chemical systems such as sugar, fat and protein metabolism. Common mental symptoms of Cushing's syndrome include depression, emotional instability, manic behavior, and memory loss.

Dr. Harvey Cushing of Johns Hopkins University discovered the syndrome that bears his name, *Cushing's Syndrome.* It is caused by too much cortisone.

The hormone is used to treat many illnesses, including asthma, arthritis, and lupus. This treatment is not without side effects, however. Prolonged treatment with cortisone can cause depression, hallucinations, delusions and dementia.

Elderly people may experience mental symptoms even with small doses of this hormone. Withdrawal from cortisone can also cause memory and mental impairment. Never stop taking this drug without a doctor's supervision.

BIRTH CONTROL PILLS

Birth control pills work by altering the hormone balance in the body. It has been claimed that up to 50% of women on the pill have some sort of mental symptoms as a result of the medication. The most common side effect is depression, which impairs memory.

Many of the side effects of oral contraceptives can be corrected by using vitamin B_6 supplementation. But the use of oral contraceptives also causes other nutritional deficiencies, including folate, zinc, and vitamin B_2, B_{12}, B_6, and C. At the same time iron, copper and vitamin A levels are often increased. These findings suggest decreased liver metabolism of these essential nutrients.

ESTROGEN

A recent study has shown that estrogen replacement therapy can improve memory and reduce symptoms in elderly women suffering from Alzheimer's disease. Although this is a preliminary study, the results were significant enough to warrant further study.

ACTH

The pituitary hormones *adrenocorticotrophic hormone* (ACTH) and *melanocyte-stimulating hormone* (MSH), when combined as ACTH/MSH, show potential as a memory-enhancing drug. Injections of this hormone combination seem to boost the power of concentration, and may be useful in treating certain types of mental retardation.

The drug is also being tested on Alzheimer's victims and patients with senility. But the drug is still experimental and has potentially dangerous side effects.

DHEA

DHEA (*Dehydroepiandrosterone*) is a naturally occurring molecule in the human body. In the body DHEA is converted into as many as twenty different steroid hormones.

Many life-extension researchers feel that DHEA is important because it is necessary for proper production of many other hormones, and because it decreases with age. The average 70 year old has one-fifth the level of DHEA they had at twenty.

DHEA appears to improve retention of information that has already been learned. Several studies have shown that the drug increases memory retention in mice.

There is some evidence that DHEA may increase the risk of prostate cancer. Becuase of this, some memory researchers feel that men should always take saw palmetto with DHEA in order to decrease this risk. No studies ave been done on the long termeffects of taking DHEA. For this reason, it should be used with caution.

DHEA is available by prescription and by mail order. Recommended dosage ranges from 25mg to 100mg per day.

VASOPRESSIN

Vasopressin, a naturally occurring substance in the brain, is also known as *antidiuretic hormone*. It is manufactured in the posterior pituitary gland, which is located at the base of the brain. The hormone is used by the body to regulate blood pressure and urine volume, but it has also been shown to have an important effect on memory.

In several interesting studies, scientists found that vaso-pressin could restore memory in amnesia victims, sometimes within minutes after their taking it. Other studies showed improved learning in men aged 50 to 60.

Cocaine releases vasopressin, but soon depletes the brain's supply of it. This is why people who go on two- or three -day cocaine binges often become psychotic. Nicotine, alcohol, and marijuana inhibit the release of vasopressin, resulting in memory impairment.

Most physicians are familiar with vasopressin only as a substance used for treating frequent urination associated with diabetes. Therefore, if you want a prescription for memory improvement, you should provide your doctor with the research papers on the use of the drug for memory improvement.

Large doses of vasopressin (several hundred Interna-tional Units) can increase blood pressure, and therefore it should be used with careful supervision. This hormone is available by prescription under the brand name *Diapid*, and comes in the form of a nasal spray.

The recommended dose for Diapid is 16 International Units per day. As a nasal spray, use one spray in each nostril 3 to 4 times per day, which is equivalent to 12-16 U.S.P. units.

MELATONIN

Melatonin is a naturally occurring hormone that is produced by the pineal gland. In the 1980s, scientists began to look at the possibility that melatonin could be used to adjust the body's biological clock.

Melatonin production declines with age. In young animals and humans the twenty four hour cycle of melatonin is very robust. However, the cycle frequently deteriorates during aging and is totally abolished in patients with neurological diseases such as Alzheimer's.

Melatonin is a highly efficient free-radical scavenger, especially of hydroxyl radicals. Dementia due to premature aging in patients with Down's syndrome, and accelerated aging in patients with Alzheimer's disease may be caused by exposure to hydroxyl radicals.

High doses (over 200 mg per day) can worsen depression and insomnia, but doses of 3 to 30 mg a day usually show no side effects. Melatonin should not be taken by patients with myelocytic leukemia or multiple myeloma.

Many of the claims made about melatonin are overblown and unsubstantiated, but melatonin can be used to relieve insomnia, to alleviate depression, and to reduce free radical damage in the body. It can also be taken to reset the body's clock to minimize jet lag.

Dosage and timing are important when using this substance, and use should be supervised by a physician.

CHAPTER SEVENTEEN

MEDICATIONS AND MEMORY

Although most people don't realize it, many over-the-counter medications interfere with memory. Yet few if any of these medications indicate memory impairment as a side effect.

Many prescription medications also grossly interfere with memory. But most doctors don't mention that the drug they are prescribing may have an effect on memory.

Most people take any medication that their doctor recommends without question. The majority of the people I work with don't know the names of the medicines they are taking, or why they are taking them.

In his book, *The People's Pharmacy,* Joe Graeden claims that many cases of senility are actually a result of the toxic effects of over-medication. He calls this problem the "spaced-out Grandma syndrome."

Over-medication is a very common problem. One woman who came to see me was taking seventeen prescription medications! These drugs were given to her by several doctors for various ailments she had suffered over a period of years, but it seemed that no one had ever asked her if she was taking any other medication. Furthermore, none of the doctors told her

DRUGS THAT CAN CAUSE MEMORY PROBLEMS

Antidepressants	Eye drops for glaucoma
Antihistamines	Glutethimide
Antipsychotics	Haloperidol (Haldol)
Atropine	Lithium Carbonate
Barbiturates	Mephenytoin
Benzodiazepines	Methyldopa
Blood Pressure medication	Misolene
Bromides	Phenytoin
Clonidine	Propranolol
Digitalis	Reserpine
Dilantin	Scopolamine
Disulfiram	Serpasil

when to stop taking the medication, so she continued to take medicine for ailments that had disappeared long ago.

The average number of prescription drugs given to people over sixty years old is *fifteen per year!* Although elderly people (those over 65) comprise 12% of the population, they take 30% of all prescribed medications. Two-thirds of this population is taking at least one prescription drug. Thirty-seven percent are taking at least five drugs. Another 20% are taking *seven or more* medications at once.

About one-third of elderly people make serious mistakes in taking their medication, either forgetting to take it, or forgetting that they have taken it, and therefore overdosing. About 12% of people taking prescription drugs are using medications that were actually prescribed for someone else. It is estimated that almost 200,000 people in this country are currently suffering from medication-induced memory loss.

The loss of brain cells and the lower amounts of neurotransmitters in the older brain amplify the effects of many medications, and doses that are safe for younger people are often toxic in the aged. Decreased liver and kidney function also increase the risk of toxicity. In short, medications should be taken with care, and closely monitored.

SLEEPING PILLS

Sleeping pills can cause confusion and memory loss. People who use sleeping pills regularly often complain that their memory is bad. Most sleeping pills contain ingredients that interfere with REM sleep, the part of sleep in which dreaming occurs. When dreaming is disrupted, long-term memory storage cannot take place. One of the more popular sleeping medications, *Halcion*, is known to cause amnesia.

Sleeping pills are meant to be used once in a while. If they are used more than three consecutive weeks, they become ineffective, because the body adjusts to them. Even though the pills no longer work, the user becomes addicted to them, and begins to believe that he cannot sleep without them. Unfortunately, the only effect the pills have is impairing memory. **If you have been taking sleeping pills for any length of time, do not stop without consulting your doctor. Sudden withdrawal from this medication can have serious consequences.**

STIMULANT DRUGS

Stimulant drugs such as Cocaine and Amphetamine cause damage to tiny blood vessels in the brain (called capillaries) and decrease the supply of nutrients and oxygen. They also deplete the brain of the neurotransmitter dopamine, which is necessary for decoding sensory input. If these drugs are used frequently, psychosis and permanent brain damage can occur.

TRANQUILIZERS

The most common treatment of anxiety is the use of tranquilizing drugs. Each year, thousands of people are given Valium and Xanax to reduce symptoms of anxiety. But not only are these drugs ineffective as a treatment, they are highly addictive. Once a person becomes addicted to tranquilizers, it is extremely difficult to get them off the drugs. Tranquilizing drugs are sedating, and interfere with memory in many ways.

If you are suffering from anxiousness, anxiety, or panic attacks, seek help from a psychologist trained in treating these disorders without medication.

CAFFEINE

Americans consume about one-third of the caffeine in the world. The average American consumes 150-225 mg of caffeine a day. The compound is a hidden ingredient in many beverages like coffee, tea, cola, over-the-counter drugs, and many stimulants and analgesics. A typical cup of coffee contains from 50 to 150 mg of caffeine. A cup of tea contains 50 mg, and a 12-ounce cola contains about 35 mg. Some people consume an excess of 7,500 mg per day.

Addiction to caffeine is sometimes called *caffeinism*. When a person becomes addicted to caffeine, they need it to function normally. If they stop using it, they suffer from fatigue, depression, and severe headaches. Excessive caffeine intake has been shown to increase the degree of mental illness in psychiatric patients, but extreme amounts of caffeine may worsen the effects of both mental and physical illness in everyone.

Caffeine stimulates the central nervous system by blocking the action of a substance called *adenosine*. Caffeine can

trigger phobias and panic attacks. It can also cause sleep disturbances. As mentioned before, sleep disturbances impair memory
storage. In sensitive individuals, one cup of coffee in the morning can disrupt sleep patterns that night. Regular coffee drinkers
do not build up a tolerance for the stressful affects of caffeine.

MARIJUANA

About 40 million Americans use marijuana daily. There is
evidence that marijuana interferes with the ability to form new
memories. The brain transmits information from cell to cell by
chemicals called neurotransmitters. These molecules jump from
one cell to another across a small space between cells called a
synapse.

Some studies suggest that long-term use of marijuana
impairs memory by increasing the distance between synapses,
making it difficult for the neurotransmitters to reach the next
cell. There is also some evidence that marijuana decreases brain
levels of acetylcholine, the neurotransmitter necessary for memory transfer.

TAGAMET

Tagamet is a popular drug used to reduce excess stomach acid.
Although it was once available only by prescription, it has been
recently declassified, and is now available over the counter.
Tagamet has been shown to cause trouble with concentration,
promote irritability, and in a few cases, cause severe headaches.

These effects are thought to be caused by the drug
robbing the body of iron. Impairing acid secretion in the stomach, the main effect of the drug, blocks the absorption of ionic
iron (the form of iron found in vegetables).

QUESTIONS TO ASK YOUR DOCTOR
ABOUT MEDICATIONS

Why do I need to take this drug?

How does it work?

How long will I have to take it?

What are the side effects of this drug?

Can this drug effect my memory in any way?

What are the effects of taking this drug for more than a year?

Will this drug interact with any of the other drugs I am taking?

What will happen if I stop taking this drug?

MINERAL OIL

This commonly used laxative prevents the absorption of the fat soluble vitamins— E, A, D, and K— by creating a physical barrier between food and the intestinal wall. People who use mineral oil regularly are preventing nutrients from entering their bodies by coating their intestines with oil. Use mineral oil sparingly. A high-fiber diet is a much more effective way to eliminate constipation.

BLOOD PRESSURE MEDICATION

Several types of blood pressure medication can cause depression and memory problems. A commonly prescribed diuretic,

Dyazide, depletes the body of folic acid. Folic acid deficiency is associated with both mental and emotional disturbance.

A physician placed on an experimental diet deficient in folic acid reported that after four months he suffered from sleeplessness and forgetfulness. These symptoms disappeared two days after the vitamin was reintroduced to his diet.

A three-to-five month supply of folic acid is stored in the human liver. Folic acid functions as a coenzyme in the manufacture of the neurotransmitters norepinephrine and serotonin.

Diuretic drugs also deplete the body of potassium. Low potassium can cause the brain's arteries to clamp down, impairing the blood flow. This contributes to clot formation and stroke. If you are taking Dyazide, make sure you are taking potassium supplements.

Two other blood pressure medications, *Inderal* and *Aldomet*, are known to significantly impair verbal memory.

SUGAR

Refined sugar accelerates the aging process. Although glucose is present in and around every cell in the body, an excess causes premature aging.

Glucose enters the blood stream from the small intestine. Some is used as fuel by the cells, and the rest is stored in the liver in the form of glycogen until it is needed later. In a healthy body, glucose level is kept constant by the hormone insulin. Cells getting too much glucose, as happens in people with diabetics, form proteins mixed with glucose called *advanced glycosylation end products* (AGE). These particles stick like glue to other molecules and cause *cross linking*. Cross linking leads to age-related problems such as cataracts, atherosclerosis, and senility. Eating candy bars and other high sugar food on a regular basis overloads the blood with sugar and sets off this process.

Researchers Cerami, Brownlee, and Ulrich have developed a drug called *aminoguanidine* which inhibits the formation of AGE's. It is currently being tried on diabetics.

BELLADONNA

Belladonna means "pretty woman" in Italian. The drug is so named because a drop of it in each eye causes the pupils to dilate, enhancing beauty. Belladonna has been used for many centuries, usually in its naturally occurring form in the plant *deadly nightshade*. Although the drug is not used as commonly as it was a century ago, currently belladonna is used to relieve symptoms of irritable bowel or spastic colon.

This drug has many side effects, one of which is interference with memory. These memory problems are caused by one of belladonna's active ingredients—scopolamine.

SCOPOLAMINE

Scopolamine originates from the plant *henbane*. This drug has been known for years to cause memory problems. Women used to be given large doses of scopolamine because it was thought to relieve the discomfort of childbirth. What it was actually doing was completely wiping out the memory of the birth! Doctors used to call this *twilight sleep*.

Scopolamine interferes with memory by blocking receptors in the hippocampus, the part of the brain used in transferring new material into long-term memory. Scopolamine is so effective in preventing memory that it is routinely used in memory experiments.

17: MEDICATIONS AND MEMORY 191

Scopolamine is an ingredient in several over-the-counter drugs, and is the active ingredient in some sleeping pills. Many people use patches containing scopolamine to relieve the symptoms of seasickness. If you are taking this drug, be aware that it prevents the learning of new material. Read the labels on sleeping and seasick pills before you take them.

CLIOQUINOL

Clioquinol is a drug that used to be a popular antidiarrheal medication. It was then found to cause *transient global amnesia,* and was banned for that use. However, the drug continues to appear as an ingredient in many creams, lotions and ointments and should never be taken internally.

CHAPTER EIGHTEEN

NEUROTOXINS AND MEMORY

A *neurotoxin* is any substance that causes damage or malfunction in the nervous system. Every day millions of people are exposed to hundreds of these powerful chemicals. The chemicals include cosmetics, food additives, pesticides, drugs, and common solvents. Acute exposure to neurotoxic chemicals causes nausea, dizziness, weakness, and blurred vision.

But subtle symptoms caused by chronic exposure—such as irritability, fatigue, confusion and memory loss—often go unnoticed. In addition, the chronic effects of neurotoxins do not show up on traditional medical tests, so doctors tell the sufferer that there is really nothing wrong with them, that what they are feeling is "stress."

In October 1989, the United States Government Subcommittee on Investigations and Oversight held hearings to explore the effects of neurotoxins in the environment. **They concluded that neurotoxic reaction was one of the top ten causes of illness in the country.**

As of this writing, the government has identified 850 neurotoxic chemicals in our environment, of which only 167 have regulatory standards imposed on their use.

Virtually any toxic chemical is capable of producing psychological symptoms, even substances that have never been investigated. For example, the role that bacterial by-products play in brain disorders hasn't been investigated, but it's likely that they have an effect on brain chemistry.

MERCURY

Quicksilver is a fascinating element. It is the only metal that occurs naturally as a liquid. While the metal itself is shiny, slippery, and elusive, its ability to poison the nervous system is clear and concrete.

More commonly known today as mercury, quicksilver is a highly neurotoxic chemical that has been poisoning people for centuries. Although mercury damages all types of human tissue, it is extremely toxic to the central nervous system. People with mercury poisoning display many of the symptoms of Alzheimer's disease. Lewis Carroll's "Mad Hatter" represented people who suffered from *erethism*, a disease caused by exposure to mercury—a chemical used in hat making.

In 1972, five thousand people died in Iraq from eating grain that was treated with a fungicide containing methyl mercury. The grain was seed corn that was treated with the fungicide, and was not meant to be eaten. However, the local people could not read the warning labels, and made bread from the contaminated seeds. Hospitals reported that 6,530 people showed symptoms of mercury poisoning.

The Chisso Factory in Minimata, Japan, used mercury as an ingredient for manufacturing vinyl chloride to make floor tiles. Between 1932 and 1968, they dumped about 100 tons of mercury into the local bay. This toxic waste was absorbed by the fish, which were then eaten by the townspeople. People in Minimata would often serve fish at every meal. By 1982, there were 1,773 reported cases of mercury poisoning in the town, which caused severe brain damage in most of its victims. Four hundred and fifty-six people died from the toxin. This poisoning was so rampant that the disorder resulting from it came to be known as *Minimata disease.*

There is a growing body of evidence that suggests dental fillings can be a potent source of mercury poisoning. Dental fillings are a mixture of mercury, silver, copper, zinc, and tin. Some researchers feel that these toxic metals leach into the body and cause nerve damage.

Germany and Sweden have banned the use of mercury in dental fillings. The majority of dentists that I have talked to are convinced that the fillings are perfectly safe, and the American Dental Association states unequivocally that dental fillings pose no threat. But despite the dental association's position, there are a growing number of dentists in this and other countries who feel that mercury fillings do have a subtle yet harmful effect on mental functioning.

The U.S. government has decided that mercury is a health threat. In 1990, the Environmental Protection Agency banned the use of mercury in latex house paint. Then, in 1988, the agency defined discarded dental amalgam as hazardous waste. It does seem odd that this substance would be considered hazardous waste when it is outside of your mouth, but perfectly safe when it's inside.

For more information about the possible toxicity of fillings, see the book, *Chronic Mercury Toxicity* by H.L. Queen, and the book *Beating Alzheimer's,* by Tom Warren. Warren claims that removing his mercury fillings (along with changes in diet and lifestyle) helped him recover from Alzheimer's, but I don't put much stock in his book. It's poorly documented and somewhat hysterical.

LEAD

Lead is one of the most common neurotoxins in our world today. Lead poisoning causes irreversible brain damage. For centuries people have been exposed to lead poisoning. Records from ancient Rome show that many people were poisoned by lead found in wine casks.

Lead is especially toxic to the growing brains of children. There is a clear and direct correlation between low I.Q. and childhood exposure to lead. Children often ingest lead by eating paint that is peeling from walls.

Though paint containing lead was banned in 1978, toxic lead is found in a multitude of places in our modern environment. In fact, it is believed that because of modern mining and manufacturing, lead levels on our environment are 500 times higher than they were in prehistoric times.

Lead soldered cans account for 14% of the lead ingestion in this country. Within five days of opening, canned juices accumulate five times the amount of lead considered safe. For this reason canned juice should be avoided. If you do use canned juice, pour it immediately into a glass container.

The FDA has discovered that coffee and tea urns in many fast food restaurants are a potent source of lead. Some older urns contain as many as 680 parts per billion (ppb), which is thirteen times the federal safety standard of 50 ppb. The EPA feels that the safety standard is too high, and wants the safe level of lead lowered to 10 ppb.

High-quality crystal has always contained lead. Joseph Graziano, Ph.D., and Conrad Blum, M.D., conducted an experiment on lead crystal. They poured port wine into crystal containers containing between 24 and 33% lead oxide. After four months, the lead content of the port was 65 times greater! The lead in the crystal containers began to leach into the wine in as little as 20 minutes, and the lead level tripled in four hours. Crystal baby bottles leach lead also, and should not be used.

Many older buildings are plumbed with lead soldered pipes, and much of ingested lead comes from drinking water from these pipes. If you would like to test your water for lead, contact the American Council of Independent Laboratories, 1629 K Street, NW, Suite 400, Washington DC 20006 (202) 887-5872. They can provide a contact in or area.

Before it was banned in 1972, gasoline containing tetra ethyl lead was responsible for pouring 220 million pounds of lead into our atmosphere. Over three billion pounds of lead were released into the air by manufacturing. Although it has been many years since lead was eliminated from gasoline, the lead particles settled into the soil where they still remain.

A group headed by Rufus Chaney from the U.S. Department of Agriculture developed a test that assesses lead levels in the soil. It is called the *Chaney-Mielke soil test*. Chaney found lead levels of 5,000 parts per million in the soil of many Maryland gardens. Normal soil should contain about 15 to 40 parts per million. Soil containing more than 500 parts per million is defined as toxic waste by the Environmental Protection Agency. It is believed that the soil in many larger cities is contaminated with lead from many years of accumulation of paint and gasoline particles.

Mr. Chaney tells me that if you would like to test the soil in your area, contact your local County Agricultural agent. For specific information on Chaney's research, contact the Environmental Chemistry Laboratory, Agricultural Research Service, U.S. Department of Agriculture, Beltsvile, MD 20705, (301) 504-8324.

In the human body, a blood level of lead above 10 micrograms (mcg) per 100 milliliters of blood are considered dangerous. People showing levels above 60mcg are said to have lead poisoning.

The most accurate test for lead levels in the body is hair analysis, except in cases of acute lead poisoning, where body fluid analysis is better. For information on hair analysis for lead, write to Doctors Data Laboratories, Inc., P.O. Box 111, 30 West 101 Roosevelt Road, West Chicago, IL 60185-9986, or call (800) 323-2784. Also contact the Leek Corporation in Costa Mesa, CA, (714) 548-5595. Dr. Richard Leek is one of the world's leading experts in accurate hair analysis.

The most effective treatment to eliminate lead from the body is *chelation therapy* (discussed in chapters 12 and 19). A new drug called *succimer* (brand named *Chemet,* and pronounced *key-met*) which also reduces lead levels, is available from Sanofu Pharmaceutical (800)-223-1062. Although this drug is used primarily for lead poisoning in children, it has been shown to be effective in adults also.

ALUMINUM

Aluminum has been found in high concentrations in the brains of people with Alzheimer's disease. At this time, researchers are uncertain about aluminum's exact role in Alzheimer's. It is not known whether aluminum is one of the causes of it, or if the disease allows aluminum to accumulate in the brain. Until all the evidence is in, it is a good idea to avoid any products containing aluminum. Autopsies done on Alzheimer's victims show that bundles of debris in the brain called *neuritic plaques*, one of the hallmarks of the disease, contain a tiny core of aluminum.

Dr. Daniel Perl claims that aluminum that is inhaled through the nose can enter the brain through the olfactory nerves, which are linked to the sense of smell. Biochemist

Eugene Roberts agrees, stating that inhaled aluminum is absorbed directly into the olfactory lobes. The most common source of inhaled aluminum is in spray deodorants, but aluminum is also present in the air in most urban areas.

Two acids contained in fruit, *citric acid* and *malic acid*, have been shown to increase excretion of aluminum in animals. Malic acid works best in eliminating aluminum from brain tissue. This substance is found in wine, apples, cherries, and other fruits.

GLUTAMATE

Scientists at Massachusetts General Hospital found that brains of Alzheimer's victims have deformed glutamate containing neurons. Monosodium glutamate (MSG) and aspartame (Nutrasweet) contain glutamate, and should be used sparingly.

NUTRASWEET

Despite its approval by the FDA, Nutrasweet, or Aspartame, has not been shown to be safe. Since 1983, Aspartame has been used in carbonated beverages. It's composed of three amino acids: aspartic acid, phenylalanine and methanol.

Aspartame can significantly affect mood and behavior. In animals, at levels comparable to those of human consumption, aspartame increases central nervous system tyrosine and phenylalanine levels while decreasing the levels of tryptophan. Tryptophan is an amino acid needed to manufacture the neurotransmitter *serotonin*. Low levels of serotonin are found in people suffering from depression. (Prozac is an antidepressant drug that works by increasing brain serotonin levels). Evidence suggests that continued use of Aspartame results in decreased serotonin levels, which can lead to depression.

The methanol portion of Aspartame could also have significant effects on the brain. Methanol is quite toxic, and the amount of methanol in one gram of Nutrasweet is 100mg. The affect of long-term intake of toxic doses of methanol has yet to be determined.

A child consuming 700mg of Nutrasweet per day is consuming 10 times the environmental protection agency's recommended daily limit for consumption of methanol.

SMOKING

Smoking affects behavior through the actions of carbon monoxide and nicotine. Smoking also causes low vitamin C levels and elevated levels of blood fats and adrenal corticosteroids. At levels typical of those of cigarette smokers, nicotine causes an altered pattern of brain waves (as measured by an EEG).

Smoking has been shown to produce a significant rise in growth hormone, cortisol, anti-diuretic hormone, norepinephrine, epinephrine and glycerol in the plasma. It increases blood pressure and pulse rate, while it decreases skeletal muscle tone, deep tension reflexes, and decreases skin temperature.

Processed tobacco contains *cadmium*, a heavy metal ten times more toxic than lead, which causes free radical damage. Smoke also carries with it small amounts of radioactive isotopes, which also promotes free radical damage.

These problems are compounded by the fact that cigarette smoking is associated with increased sugar and caffeine consumption. The effect of this combination is *reactive hypoglycemia*, which can lead to both depression and memory problems. There is no question that smoking is harmful. Stop now.

ALCOHOL

It's been said that some drink to remember while others drink to forget. But the odds are that forgetting is the more likely result.

Alcohol is metabolized in the body into a chemical called *acetaldehyde,* which then creates free radicals. Acetaldehyde is a close relative of *formaldehyde* (embalming fluid) which causes cross linkage of connective tissue. This is the same chemical reaction that is used in tanning hides and browning food.

Chronic alcoholism is a major cause of memory and mental disorders. Chronic alcohol intake destroys brain cells. If the damage is continuous over a period of time, a condition known as *Korsakoff's psychosis* results. The main symptom of this disorder is severe memory loss. People with Korsakoff's have amnesia for past and present events. They attempt to cover up their memory loss by making things up, a process known as *confabulation.* Constant drinking results in many nutritional deficiencies including shortages of vitamin A, B-complex, vitamin E and C, magnesium, selenium and zinc. Many experts feel that adding vitamins to beer would help prevent this disease.

Although it is clear that long-term heavy drinking damages the brain, even moderate drinking impairs memory storage. Long-term memory is not impaired while a person is drinking. Drunk people still remember who they are and details about their life. But things experienced while a person is drunk are not remembered later on when they are sober. About two-thirds of alcoholics experience complete "blackouts," a total loss of memory for events that occur while the individual is drunk.

Alcohol can impair memory performance up to fourteen hours after ingesting it. Studies show that in general, heavy drinkers do worse on memory tasks than light drinkers.

Recent research has linked alcohol to several types of brain damage. Rats given alcohol show damage to the *hippocampus*, the part of the brain responsible for memory storage.

There is also evidence that alcohol damages the *cerebellum*, the part of the brain responsible for fine motor movement and balance. Some heavy drinkers of Italian *Chianti* suffer damage to the *corpus callosum*, the connection between the brain's hemispheres.

There is also mounting evidence that a person's overall nutritional status has an effect on alcohol consumption, that is, proper nutrition may prevent alcoholism. In a study done on nutrition and drinking, people placed on a diet high in raw foods began to spontaneously avoid alcohol and smoking. Alcoholics placed on the same diet had a much higher abstinence rate than subjects in the control group.

In another study, rats fed a junk-food diet continuously increased alcohol consumption, while another group fed a highly nutritious diet showed no escalation. Interestingly, when the rats were given caffeine, *both groups* increased alcohol consumption. This is something every AA chapter should consider. Rats made deficient in B vitamins chose alcohol over water. While their preference was reversed when they were given B vitamins.

In another study, thirty two people with high blood pressure were fed 62% of their calories in the form of raw foods for six months. As a result of the change in diet, 80% of the people in the study spontaneously stopped using alcohol and tobacco!

The amino acid *L-glutamine* has been shown to reduce the craving for alcohol. *Evening Primrose Oil,* an extract of the Primrose, which contains high levels of *gamma linoleic acid*, also reduces the craving for alcohol, by preventing tolerance to the drug.

The nutrients *DL-carnitine, catechin, gamma linoleic acid, glutathione* and *panthetine* all appear to protect the liver from damage by alcohol. But taking these supplements does not replace the need to minimize alcohol intake.

The precursors of *prostaglandin E1* may lessen alcohol withdrawal symptoms, while *nicotinic acid* and *pantethine* have the ability to reduce *acetaldehyde*, a toxic chemical formed by the metabolic breakdown of alcohol.

In addition to the above effects of drinking, chronic alcohol consumption causes destruction of the liver, leading to a condition called *cirrhosis*. Even very early liver failure results in inability of the body to store vitamin A. This is true even when serum levels are normal. Vitamin A and zinc deficiencies cause night blindness, impaired immune function, and loss of taste and smell, which can lead to loss of the desire to eat. This loss of desire to eat then results in many nutritional deficiencies.

When damage occurs, the liver can no longer metabolize nutrients or eliminate toxins from the body. Liver disease leads to the failure of protein synthesis, reduced zinc, and decreased ability to store vitamin B_6 and vitamin A.

Still another reason to avoid alcohol is that chronic consumption causes nutritional problems because of *gastritis,* an irritation of the lining of the stomach and intestines which causes anorexia and vomiting. Irritation of the small intestine leads to chronic diarrhea, resulting in electrolyte imbalances and the failure to absorb nutrients. All of the body's systems then malfunction, including memory systems.

The increase in stomach acid that occurs when drinking may cause increased insulin release, which leads to reactive hypoglycemia, a temporary drop in blood sugar.

Nutritional researchers have discovered a link between nicotinic acid (a form of vitamin B_3) and alcohol addiction. When alcohol is broken down in the body, it is converted into the chemical *acetaldehyde*. In the brain, this chemical combines with the neurotransmitter dopamine to form a substance known as *tetrahydropapoveroline*. Tetrahydropapoveroline is a morphine like substance that may be a contributing cause for alcohol addiction. Nicotinic acid interferes in the production of Tetrahydropapoveroline, and therefore reduces the craving for alcohol. The recommended dose is 500mg a day.

Vitamin B_{12} is essential for normal memory functioning. However, the liver content of B_{12} in alcoholics has been found to be low, even though blood levels of the vitamin were high.

This and other studies suggest that B_{12} levels may be low in tissues even though they appear normal in blood tests. In fact, several studies show that serum B_{12} levels are actually higher in alcoholics even though their brain and tissue levels are significantly low. This occurs because the damaged liver cannot absorb and metabolize the B_{12}.

There are several groups and organizations that specialize in the treatment of alcoholism through nutrition. Joan Larson has developed a program which is available in her book, *Seven Weeks to Sobriety*. The book can be ordered from Bio-Recovery, Inc., 3255 Hennipin Avenue South, Minneapolis, MN 55408, (800) 247-6237.

Other information can be obtained from California Recovery Systems, Mill Valley, CA, (415) 383-3611, Milan Recovery Programs, Seattle, WA, (206) 241-0890, and Comprehensive Medical Care, Amityville, NY, (516) 598-2960.

CHAPTER NINETEEN

FREE RADICALS AND ANTIOXIDANTS

The car came out of nowhere. The young boy was thrown from his bike and knocked unconscious. When the paramedics arrived, they immediately put an oxygen mask over his face.

Oxygen is absolutely essential to life. Paramedics are quick to give injured people oxygen because the brain can survive only a few moments without it. Oxygen does its work in the body by combining with other molecules through a process called *oxidation.* This is the same reaction that causes iron to rust.

But even though oxygen is essential to life, it is also involved in chemical processes that can damage the body. Certain chemical reactions in the body create a chemical called *singlet state oxygen,* which can cause damage to cells.

The human body is composed of millions of complex molecules. Molecules in the body are said to be stable when the electrons attached to them exist in pairs. When one of these electrons is missing, as is the case with singlet state oxygen, the resulting molecule is called a *free radical.*

Free radicals are highly reactive molecules in the body that rapidly combine with other molecules. The missing electron allows a free radical to react with any substance in its vicinity. Free radicals quickly steal electrons from other molecules, and damage the molecules in the process. Free radicals create abnormally functioning cells that die or mutate into cancerous tissue.

Furthermore, when a free radical steals an electron, it starts a chain reaction that creates thousands of other free radicals. DNA and RNA, which are the molecules that make up our genes, are very vulnerable to free radical damage.

Free radicals come from inside and outside of the body. For example, white blood cells in the body generate thousands of free radicals that help destroy invading germs, while sunlight, X rays, radiation, and environmental pollutants are external sources of free radicals. The harmful effects of radiation (X rays, ultraviolet rays, and gamma rays) occur because photons of radiation knock electrons out of orbit, creating free radicals in the body.

In addition to attack by environmental factors, lifestyle plays an important role in free radical production. Smoking creates a large amount of free radicals, and high levels of stress can induce this type of damage.

Fat is also a contributor. The average human can consume 20% of calories in the form of fat without upsetting the body's free radical protection system. But the average American now consumes over 40% of his or her calories from fat. High fat diets produce millions of free radicals, and are a major cause of cancer.

Research in senility, dementia and stroke incriminates free radicals as a major cause of nerve damage. In fact, Alzheimer's and other dementias are thought by some researchers to be largely the result of free radical damage.

ANTIOXIDANTS

Antioxidants are substances that seek out and neutralize free radicals by combining with them. For this reason, these compounds are also called *free radical scavengers*. They gobble up free radicals, and prevent damage to the body.

Catecholamines are important chemicals that transmit information from one neuron to another. They produce free radicals when the catecholamines are broken down after use.

In a healthy brain, these free radicals are removed by the free radical scavengers. But if the nervous system's free radical defense system is impaired, the receptors on the neurons can be damaged. This damage may lead to Parkinson's disease, and possibly some types of schizophrenia.

Proper amounts of oxygen in the body help to prevent free radicals. Exercise increases oxygen uptake, resulting in adequate oxygenation of capillary beds, the tiny blood vessels that feed oxygen to cells. Other ways to reduce free radical damage include reducing the amount of animal fat in the diet, and avoiding *nitrites,* toxic chemicals that are found in bacon and other prepared meats.

VITAMINS AND NUTRIENTS

The antioxidants that are especially important in slowing brain aging include vitamin E, vitamin C (both the water and fat soluble types), beta carotene, selenium and melatonin. These substances are discussed elsewhere in this book, but several other interesting antioxidants are explored here.

BIOFLAVINOIDS

Albert Szent-Gyorgyi, the man who first synthesized vitamin C, discovered that an impurity in his preparation had the ability to stop bleeding. The "impurity" turned out to be a family of chemicals called *bioflavinoids*. Bioflavinoids are not classified as vitamins, because they are not considered to be essential for life. However, they play important roles in health and well-being. They are powerful antioxidants, and they protect the liver from damage from environmental toxins.

Most importantly for our purposes, they prevent capillary damage and therefore significantly reduce the risk of stroke. Good sources of these chemicals are apples, the white part of citrus fruits, tea and onions.

GLUTATHIONE AND CYSTEINE

Glutathione is a substance produced in the body that acts as a powerful antioxidant. The level of glutathione in the blood is proportional to the amount of cysteine in the body, so more cysteine means more glutathione. In addition, cysteine possesses the ability to eliminate heavy metals from the body.

PROANTHOCYANIDINS (PAC)

One of the most potent antioxidants found in nature is a class of bioflavonoids called *proanthocyanadins* (PAC). Until recently the high cost of extracting these chemicals has kept many people from using them. But there are now inexpensive processes which can extract proanthocynadins from grape seeds and from pine bark.

Some nutritionists claim that proanthocyanadins are the most effective natural antioxidants yet discovered.

The makers of grape seed extract claim that it contains 95% proanthocyanidins and is less expensive than *pycnogenol,* the substance that is extracted from pine. Still another source of proanthocyanadins is *European bilberry.*

It was Professor J. Masquelier who first patented the pine bark extract in 1951. He also patented grape seed extract in 1986. But the original source of PACs was actually from peanuts, discovered by him in 1948.

Proanthocyanadins are rapidly absorbed and distributed throughout the body within minutes of ingestion. They readily cross the blood-brain barrier to provide immediate antioxidant activity to the central nervous system.

These substances are claimed to have antioxidant properties 50 times greater than vitamin E, and 20 times greater than vitamin C. They restore the antioxidant status of oxidized vitamin C, and help transport vitamin C into cells.

Proanthocyanadins are also said to increase the elasticity and flexibility of *collagen,* which helps restore the connective tissue underlying the skin to a more youthful structure. They also act as a smooth muscle relaxant in the blood vessels.

A single 100 milligram dose of PAC increases capillary resistance by 140%.This means that it strengthens the walls of the capillaries. This same treatment has been shown to reduce cholesterol by 30%. Dr. Richard Passwater in his book *Supernutrition,* claims these substances are effective in treating senility.

GREEN TEA

In numerous studies, green tea has been shown to reduce the incidence of cancer, heart disease, stroke, hypertension and infections. The active components of green tea are substances called *polyphenols.*

Dr. Brian Leibowitz in the *Journal of Optimal Health*, states "...polyphenols are a remarkable group of naturally occurring non-toxic molecules which hold tremendous promise for the prevention and treatment of a variety of diseases including allergy, asthma, inflammation, cancer, infectious diseases, diabetic cataracts, alcoholic hepatitis and other liver diseases, and cardiovascular disease."

MILK THISTLE EXTRACT

Milk thistle extract contains 85.6% of a substance called *silymarin,* an antioxidant that is said to have a beneficial effect on liver function. Silymarin protects and enhances liver function through its ability to stimulate liver protein synthesis and deters liver damage from such factors as free radicals, poisons and pollutants.

BARLEY AND WHEAT GRASS JUICE

Organic barley and wheat grass juice are rich in natural vitamin C, beta-carotene, potassium, magnesium and calcium.

Barley juice has also been used successfully to treat arthritis. Its exact mechanism of action is not known. However, life extension doctor Julian Whitaker, in his newsletter *Health And Healing*, states that he has added dried barley and wheat grass juice to his recommended list of everyday supplements. Whitaker says that he has observed significant improvements in arthritis patients who consume barley and wheat grass juice powders.

Wheat grass juice comes only from wheat sprouts, and therefore, has no wheat allergens. Wheat grass functions as a blood purifier and as a cleansing agent for cells because of the abundant amount of chlorophyll it contains.

These juices are also thought to stimulate the production of *superoxide dismutase* (SOD), a powerful free radical scavenger.

Superoxide dismutase is the fifth most prevalent molecule in the human body. According to Dr. Richard Cutler of the National Institute on Aging, the life span of man is directly proportional to SOD content. In youth, the liver produces 1700 units of SOD per gram of body weight each day, but by age 80, the production of SOD drops to less than 50 units per gram.

Gerontological researchers have for years been looking for an effective method for increasing SOD levels. Wheat sprouts, along with barley and wheat grass juices contain abundant amounts of SOD and other antioxidant enzymes. These natural antioxidant enzymes have also been shown to alleviate the symptoms of chronic arthritis.

Peter R. Rothschild, M.D., Ph.D., has found that when large amounts of SOD are taken orally, much of it survives all the way to the bloodstream within one hour of consumption. Dr. Rothschild demonstrated that SOD can be absorbed by bonding with lecithin to form an emulsified "liposome" that is assimilated through the small veins in the small intestine.

If Rothschild is correct, and the SOD found in barley and wheat grass juice actually does survive into the blood stream in this form, it would be one of the most effective anti-aging substances known.

ROYAL JELLY AND BEE POLLEN

Royal jelly and bee pollen are loaded with antioxidant vitamins. There is also a high concentration of pantothenic acid in these substances. Royal jelly is thought to contribute to the longevity of the queen bee, who far outlives all the other bees in a hive.

Bee pollen contains high amounts of SOD and is a powerful source of vitamins, minerals and coenzymes.

EDTA

Chelation therapy uses a drug known as EDTA, which is a chemical that some believe can reduce the production of free radicals as much as a millionfold. It binds ionic metal catalysts making them chemically inert and removes them from the body.

HYPERBARIC OXYGEN THERAPY

Hyperbaric oxygen therapy (HBO) is a controversial treatment that is claimed to stop free radical damage due to brain injury. For the greatest effectiveness the treatment should begin within thirty minutes of injury to the brain, but proponents claim that it helps even months after the injury.

The therapy consists of intermittent exposures of 100% oxygen at up to twice normal atmospheric pressure. This is said to interrupt free radical damage. Oxygen in properly controlled doses is an excellent free radical scavenger. Lack of oxygen, which results from an impaired blood supply, increases free radical reactions.

Hyperbaric oxygen raises oxygen tension to normal levels in damaged tissues. It also stimulates an increase of free radical scavenging enzymes such as superoxide dismutase (SOD).

Rebound dilation of blood vessels occurs following HBO which improves blood flow to affected organs. HBO also kills disease causing organisms such as anaerobic bacteria, and stimulates the growth of new blood vessels.

HBO protects the fatty sheaths surrounding nerve tracts in the brain and spinal column from free radical damage, relieving symptoms of stroke, senility and multiple sclerosis. It is most effective in the early stages of these conditions.

This treatment must be done carefully, as too much oxygen is just as damaging as too little. For more information on hyperbaric oxygen therapy, contact the Steenblock Institute 26381 Crown Valley Pkwy, Suite 130, Mission Viejo, CA. 92691, (714) 367-8870.

CHAPTER TWENTY

DRUGS THAT IMPROVE MEMORY

In the past few years, scientists have begun to explore a new class of drugs that improve or enhance memory. Some of these drugs improve memory problems caused by age and illness. Others can actually improve memory in normal, healthy people. These drugs are called *nootropics*, a term which comes from the Greek words *noos* (mind) and *tropein* (toward). In the popular press they are called *smart drugs*.

ADRAFINIL

This substance increases alertness without interfering with sleep. After about fifteen days of use, there is an increase in energy, and after about three months, intellectual function is enhanced.

DMAE

DMAE (Dimethylaminoethanol) was once marketed as the prescription drug *Deaner*, and was used to treat hyperactivity. It is a building block of the neurotransmitter acetylcholine. It is also an antioxidant free-radical scavenger.

DMAE is found naturally in sardines and anchovies. Vitamin Research Products makes a mixture called *I.Q. Plus* which contains DMAE, choline, lecithin, phosphatydyl choline, ginkgo biloba, and vitamin B_5. Their phone number is 800 VRP-24-Hr.

The recommended dosage is from 250 to 1,000mg per day, which is usually taken in the morning. Every person must establish their own effective dose level. It usually takes several weeks to experience the effects. DMAE does have side effects, and can produce insomnia, headaches, muscle tension and depression. I personally have used DMAE and find that it makes me anxious and depressed, but other people report good results with it.

HYDERGINE

Hydergine is the first drug ever to have a positive effect on people with Alzheimer's disease. Hydergine is one of a family of drugs called *hydrogenated ergot alkaloids.*

Ergot is a fungus that grows on rye. Practitioners of folk medicine often used ergot to lower blood pressure in mothers during childbirth. It was this effect on blood pressure that led the Sandoz company to research the family of chemicals found in ergot. From this research came Hydergine. Hydergine is actually the brand name used by the Sandoz Company. Other brand names of Hydergine are *Deapril-ST* and *Circanol.*

Hydergine affects brain function in several ways. It normalizes systolic blood pressure, lowers cholesterol, reduces dizziness, and decreases ringing in the ears (tinnitus). The drug also acts as a central nervous system stimulant, increases the brain's capacity to use oxygen, boosts the blood supply to the brain, enhances metabolism in brain cells, and improves memory and learning. There is evidence that Hydergine also slows the accumulation of the age pigment *lipofuscin* in brain cells.

One of the most important effects of Hydergine is that it protects brain cells from damage from oxygen starvation. It also inhibits damage from free radicals.

Even though Hydergine has been shown to exhibit all of the above effects, it is used in the United States only to treat senility and poor blood circulation to the brain (which is responsible for many of the symptoms of senility).

In their book, *Life Extension*, bio-chemical researchers Durk Pearson and Sandy Shaw state that many people fail to get results from Hydergine because they do not take it long enough. The drug usually begins to work within six months, but may take as long as two years before the benefits are experienced.

Hydergine may work by imitating the action of a chemical in the body called *nerve growth factor* (NGF). NGF has been shown to increase the growth of dendrites, the tiny branches at the end of nerve cells that enable one neuron to communicate with another. These connections are where memory and learning take place.

In Europe, the approved dose is 9mg. But at the present time in the United States the FDA has limited the approved dosage to 3mg., even though there are no negative side effects from higher doses. Studies show that patients receiving higher doses of the drug actually show more improvement.

Hydergine is useful, but it is not a miracle drug. Most people show slight to moderate improvement on the drug, and it works best on people with mild mental deterioration.

Too large an initial dose of Hydergine can cause nausea, headache, or gastro-intestinal upset. A large overdose of Hydergine may in fact cause amnesia like symptoms.

CENTROPHENOXINE

Centrophenoxine (brand-named *Lucidril*) is used throughout Europe to reverse the aging process. Like Hydergine, it appears to remove and prevent further accumulation of a substance called *lipofuscin* in brain cells, and improves memory and mental acuity. First synthesized in 1958, it has been shown to increase mental stamina in humans. This drug is a combination of DMAE (discussed earlier) and *Auxin,* a plant hormone. It is also a potent enemy of *hydroxyl radicals*, the most dangerous of free radicals.

Lucidril is available in 500mg tablets. The recommended dose is from 1,000 to 3,000mg per day. Increased alertness and a sense of stimulation occur soon after ingestion.

PIRACETAM

Piracetam was the first medicine to be called nootropic. It enhances cognition and mental performance, but not mood or behavior.

Marketed since 1972, it is registered in eighty six countries under a variety of names. This drug appears to enhance dopamine and acetylcholine levels. This substance is not marketed in U.S. because the patent has expired.

Piracetam is a central nervous system stimulant which appears to have no side effects and no contraindications. It is similar in molecular structure to the amino acid *pyroglutamate*. It appears to selectively affect the cerebral hemispheres. It affects the cells of the cortex by stimulating the production of *ATP* (an energy-producing chemical found in all cells), which increases the rate of metabolism and energy level of brain cells. It also appears to increase protein synthesis in the brain, and protects the brain from oxygen starvation.

Piracetam enhances learning and memory. In 1976, researchers Dimond and Bowers found that a group of students using 4.8 grams of Piracetam daily had a significant improvement in memory for verbal material. Piracetam somehow facilitates the transfer of information between the two halves of the brain, and for this reason has been used in the treatment of dyslexia. This substance also prevents memory loss from physical injury to the brain. There is also evidence that Piracetam can minimize the damage from stroke. The recommended dosage is from 2,400 to 4,800mg daily, divided into three equal doses.

L059

Still experimental, this drug is a derivative of Piracetam. Thomas Crook, Ph.D., of the Memory Assessment Clinic in Bethesda, Maryland states that this drug is particularly effective with age-associated memory impairment. It is most useful in people over 50 who have memory problems with no signs of disease. This substance may slow progression of Alzheimer's disease. It is ten times more potent than Piracetam.

L-DOPA

The neurotransmitter dopamine affects sex drive, movement, the immune system, and mood. There is evidence that schizophrenia may be caused by disruption of the neurotransmitter activity of dopamine. Parkinson's disease is caused by damage to dopamine-producing cells in the brain.

The prescription drug L-DOPA helps the brain manufacture dopamine. This drug has been shown to increase the life span of lab animals by as much as 50%. It is also an antioxidant.

VINPOCETINE

Vinpocetine is a derivative of *vincamine*, an extract of the periwinkle. Marketed in Europe under the brand name *Cavinton*, vinpocetine enhances memory in several ways. It enhances the capillary blood flow in the brain, ATP production, and utilization of glucose and oxygen in the brain. This drug is used for treatment of cerebral circulatory disorders, dizziness and other inner ear problems, and headaches.

In a study done in Hungary, 62% of patients with various neurological disorders showed clinical improvement when given vinpocetine. In another study, subjects showed improvement in short-term memory within an hour of taking the drug.

CLONIDINE

This drug has shown some promise in improvement in memory of patients with Korsakoff's psychosis, a brain disease caused by alcohol abuse.

DEPRENYL

Deprenyl, is also known under the brand names, *Jumex*, *Eldepryl*, *Movergan*, and *Selegiline*. It is actually closely related in structure to *phenylethylamine* (PEA), a substance found in chocolate which has been said to have antidepressant qualities, and which is discussed elsewhere in this book. Deprenyl inhibits an important chemical called *B-type monoamine oxidase* (MAO-B), an enzyme found in the glial cells of the brain. This enzyme's activity significantly increases with age, and is linked to depression.

At this time, Deprenyl is the only MAO-B inhibitor in clinical use, and it's the only MAO inhibitor that can be given without dietary restrictions. (Other MAO inhibitors require that you eliminate tyramine from your diet. This substance is found in cheese and wine.)

Deprenyl also enhances superoxide dismutase (SOD). This effect is unrelated to its effect on MAO-B and the inhibitory effects of the drug on neurotransmitter uptake.

Deprenyl is widely used in treating Parkinson's disease, and appears to improve symptoms in people with Alzheimer's disease. It is the only drug known to affect a part of the brain called the *substantia nigra* which seems to play a part in the ability to control movement. Researchers believe that the drug is also useful in treating Alzheimer's and in enhancing memory.

PHOSPHATIDYLSERINE

Studies show that phosphatidylserine increases memory by increasing glucose metabolism and increasing the number of neurotransmitter sites. This molecule is found on the surface of every brain cell membrane.

The effect of this drug can last up to a month after it is given. It has also been shown to relieve depression. A recent study done in Germany showed that this substance improved brain function in people with early signs of Alzheimer's.

In 1991, an Italian study showed memory improvement in seventy Alzheimer's patients given the drug for three months. A study done by the National Institute of Mental Health showed memory improvement in 150 people suffering from age associated memory impairment. It is most effective when used in people who are just beginning to show signs of the disorder.

QUINONES

For several years, research scientist Paul Gallop has been studying a family of molecules called *quinones*. Quinones are found in many fruits and vegetables, but they are also found in human cerebrospinal fluid. It's not clear whether quinones originate from the food we eat or if they are manufactured in the body.

Quinones are involved in connective tissue growth and brain metabolism. There is evidence that quinones protect against aging problems such as liver damage, cataracts, stroke, dementia, and memory impairment. Quinine may also protect tissues from free radical damage.

A quinone called *idebinone* seems to protect brain cells from damage from loss of blood supply, as in stroke. The drug delayed the onset of amnesia in rats whose blood supply was reduced from 60 ml/sec to 130 ml/sec.

When given seven days in a row after the blood supply was reduced, idebinone significantly improved learning capabilities in the rats.

In human studies, Idebinone was given to seven elderly individuals for two months. Their scores on the dementia rating scale improved as much as five points.

Researchers think that quinones may retard the slowing of cerebral energy metabolism that accompanies aging. Studies show that idebinone prevents damage to brain cell mitochondria, where fuel is converted to energy.

There is evidence that heavy alcohol consumption reduces quinone levels. In one study, thirty alcoholic patients had half the blood quinone levels of non drinking people.

Idebinone is closely related to Co-Enzyme Q_{10}, a nutrient that is found in high concentrations in the human heart. In the body, CoQ_{10} plays an important role in creating ATP (Adenosine triphosphate) which is the body's main source of energy. Although CoQ_{10} does some remarkable things, it has been shown in some studies to create free radicals. Idebinone does not.

Idebinone is a potent antioxidant, and in animal studies, has been shown to reduce brain damage from strokes. It also protects brain cells from oxygen starvation (a condition called *hypoxia*).

One human study suggests that idebinone increased the levels of serotonin (a neurotransmitter involved in mood and memory) in dementia patients.

Idebinone is now marketed under the brand name *Avan*. It is considered to be a *cerebral metabolism enhancer* effective for combating intellectual impairment in patients with dementia and Alzheimer's disease.

ASPIRIN and other NSAIDS

Recently 210 Alzheimer's patients in the Johns Hopkins Alzheimer's Disease Research Center were compared to patients taking non-steroidal anti-inflammatory drugs (NSAIDs) or aspirin on a daily basis. The patients were tested on clinical, cognitive, and psychiatric measures.

The patients taking NSAIDs performed better on three commonly used tests for mental functioning—the Mini-Mental Status Examination, the Boston Naming Test, and the delayed condition of the Benton Visual Retention Test. At the end of one year the people taking NSAIDs had less mental decline than the non-NSAID group in measures of verbal fluency, spatial recognition, and orientation.

These results suggest that NSAIDs play a protective role in Alzheimer's disease, and may delay both its onset and its progression.

WHERE TO BUY SMART DRUGS

Although smart drugs are not available in the U.S., they can be purchased from many sources. Here are a few.

International Aging Systems
PO Box 2995A Muswell Hill
London N10 2NA England
FAX 011-44-181-444-8272

Vipharm (OL,. Skouvara & Co.)
35, Agorakritoy Street,
104-40 Athens, Greece
Fax: 011-30-1-883-1680

World Health Services
PO Box 20
CH-2822 Courroux, Switzerland

International Merchandise Procurement
PO Box 336, Phuket 83000, Thailand
Fax: 011-66-76-381057

Baxamed Switzerland
Realpstrasse 83
CH-1054 Basel, Switzerland
Phone: 011-41-61-302-9066
Fax: 011-41-61-301-3872

The Cognitive Enhancement Research Institute (CERI) publishes *Smart Drugs News*, which is a great source of current information on smart drugs. They can be reached at (415) 321-CERI or FAX (415) 323-3864.

CHAPTER TWENTY-ONE

VITAMINS THAT IMPROVE MEMORY

VITAMIN C AND BRAIN FUNCTION

Vitamin C is a powerful antioxidant and free radical scavenger. The human brain is literally bathed in vitamin C. Human cerebrospinal fluid contains 100 times the concentration of vitamin C than other body fluids. It is kept in this high concentration by a biological vitamin C pump.

A study done in England showed that many geriatric patients suffered mental confusion due to a vitamin C deficiency. In another study, students with high vitamin C levels scored higher on an I.Q. test than those with low levels. When the low level group was given vitamin C for six months, their scores improved by 3.54 points.

Jeffrey Bland reported a study in which matched students with high serum vitamin C levels had I.Q.s almost five points higher than those with low serum levels. When both groups were given vitamin C (a glass of orange juice daily for six months), the high I.Q. group showed minimal improvement while the low group increased their I.Q. by 3.54 points. Retarded children showed a rise in I.Q. of up to twenty points when given the vitamin.

Although most animals manufacture vitamin C in their bodies, humans lack an enzyme necessary for its manufacture. Therefore, all of our vitamin C comes from our diet.

Because vitamin C is water soluble, it is not stored in the body, and must be replaced every day. If you are taking barbiturates, tetracycline, aspirin, cortisone, antacids or estrogen on a regular basis, you need more vitamin C. Stress and illness also increase the need for this vitamin.

There is a fat soluble form of vitamin C called *ascorbyl palmitate*. In this fat soluble form, vitamin C is more able to enter the fatty parts of the brain and prevent free radical damage. I have tried this form of the vitamin, and found that it made me nervous and jumpy, but others have reported that they tolerate it well.

A new form of vitamin C, called *Ester C*, has recently shown promise in preventing and reversing cardiovascular disease. Some researchers claim it can reduce arterial plaque by 50%. This type of vitamin C is readily absorbed into all body tissues. It is available in most health food stores.

The RDA of vitamin C is 45 mg a day, but most nutrition experts recommend at least 1000 mg a day.

VITAMIN E

Lipofuscin is an age pigment found in skin and brain cells. When this pigment collects in skin cells it shows up as "liver spots." Lipofuscin in a brain cell disrupts the cell's activity and can lead to the death of the cell. Some of the drugs in this book, such as Hydergine and Centrophenoxine, remove lipofuscin.

Both of these drugs are discussed in chapter 20. But vitamin E has also been shown to reduce the accumulation of the pigment.

David Schubert, Ph.D., at the Salk Institute for Biological Studies in San Diego claims that exposing brain cells to vitamin E in the laboratory protects them from the effects of a stroke. The vitamin's protective effect comes from its ability to limit the number of cells damaged by glutamic acid. Schubert has also shown that bathing brain cells in vitamin E protects them from a toxic protein found in amyloid plaques—the plaques that cause Alzheimer's disease.

In addition, Dr. Marguerite Kay, in the *Proceedings of the National Academy of Sciences,* has reported that vitamin E protects both the immune and nervous systems.

The difficulty with using vitamin E for these purposes is that it doesn't easily cross the blood-brain barrier, a natural protective mechanism that protects te brain from toxins. Because of this, Schubert and his colleagues are attempting to attach vitamin E to steroid-like molecules so that it more readily crosses this barrier. Although it's too early to conclude that vitamin E can actually ward off Alzheimer's, Dr. Schubert believes that there is enough evidence to warrant taking the vitamin.

Vitamin E is actually a group of related chemicals called *tocopherols.* Alpha tocopherol is the most useful to the body. Research has shown that natural vitamin E is, in fact, more active than synthetic forms. The effective dosage is 400 IU a day, and should not exceed 800 IU a day.

BETA-CAROTENE

Beta-carotene (also called *provitamin A*) is a food substance that is turned into vitamin A by an enzyme in your body. It is also an antioxidant and free radical scavenger. Beta-carotene is preferable to vitamin A because it is less toxic. The adult daily supplement range for beta-carotene is from 10,000 to 50,000 International Units a day.

FOLIC ACID

Research suggests that a deficiency in folic acid is associated with mental and emotional disturbance. In a recent study, a physician placed on a diet deficient in folic acid reported that after four months he suffered from sleeplessness and forgetfulness. These symptoms disappeared two days after supplementation with folic acid. A study of teenagers revealed that up to 85% of them got less than one third of the MDR of folic acid in their diets. Folic acid functions as a coenzyme in the manufacture of norepinephrine and serotonin.

DRUGS THAT INTERFERE WITH FOLIC ACID ABSORPTION
Antacids
Anti-inflammatories
Anticonvulsants
Aspirin
Azulfidine
Birth control pills
Anti Cholesterol drugs
Diuretics
Gold Shots
Methotrexate

B VITAMINS AND BRAIN FUNCTION

Vitamin B$_1$ (Thiamin)

A study by Ruth Flynn Farrel at the Presbyterian Children's home in Lynchberg, VA. showed that B$_1$ improved brain function. She noticed that the recovery of an accident victim suffering from aphasia (the inability to speak) was speeded up by the addition of vitamin B$_1$ in his diet. Based on this observation, she decided to add vitamin B$_1$ supplements to the diets of three retarded children who could not talk. Once placed on the B$_1$ supplements, two of the children learned to speak.

Impressed by these results, Dr. Farrel then did a double-blind study with two groups of children matched in mental ability. The group given two milligrams of B_1 scored from 7 to 87% higher than the group given a placebo.

Researcher Bruno Mind found that a stimulated nerve cell gives off eighty times the amount of B_1 than a cell at rest. This suggests that the more mental activity you engage in, the more of this vitamin you need. B_1 is also an antioxidant, and protects the brain against the harmful effects of smoking.

Chronic alcoholics often suffer from a memory disorder called *Korsakoff's psychosis*, caused by a deficiency of vitamin B_1. People with this disease have severe memory problems, and often make up stories to fill the gaps in their memory, an activity called *confabulation*.

When Dr. John Blass, director of the Dementia Research Service at the Burke Medical Research Institute, gave people with Alzheimer's symptoms 1,000 mg of thiamin three times a day for three months, their memory improved slightly. In another study researchers found that participants improved when they took 5,000 mg of thiamin per day.

Vitamin B2 (Riboflavin)

Riboflavin is important to *myelin*, the fatty substance that insulates nerve cells. Alcoholics and people who use oral contraceptives are often deficient in this substance.

Vitamin B3 (Niacin, Niacinamide)

Deficiency in this vitamin can contribute to depression, fatigue, and short-term memory problems. Niacin has been used as a tranquilizer, and in the treatment of schizophrenia.

A recent study has shown that 141 mg of niacin per day improved memory from 10 to 40%. This vitamin has also been used for increased blood circulation, as it has the ability to dilate blood vessels.

Vitamin B5 (Pantothenic acid)

Pantothenic acid is required for the conversion of choline and lecithin into the neurotransmitter acetylcholine. It is also involved in the cell's energy cycle, called the *citric acid cycle*, and acts as a metabolic stimulant.

Vitamin B6 (Pyridoxine)

Lack of B_6 can cause convulsions. But an excess can cause peripheral nerve damage. An adequate amount is needed to manufacture the neurotransmitter noradrenaline. The requirement for this vitamin can be from 5 to 400 mg per day.

Vitamin B12 (Cyanocobalamin)

Of all B vitamins, B_{12} is the most essential to memory. It is needed for the manufacture of RNA, which is involved in the memory storage process. People with B_{12} deficiencies often feel tired, inattentive, confused and forgetful. Although B_{12} deficiency is very common, especially in people over 50, it is often hard to detect because cellular deficiencies of B_{12} may occur even when blood levels appear normal.

The vitamin calms manic patients and relieves depression. H.L. Newbold, a New York nutritionist, found that B_{12} also alleviated ulcers and insomnia.

The best way to take the vitamin is in a readily absorbable form called *sublingual B_{12},* a pill placed under the tongue.

CHAPTER TWENTY-TWO

MINERALS THAT IMPROVE MEMORY

Although most minerals are found in very small concentrations in the body, they play a vitally important role in maintaining good health and sound memory.

CHROMIUM

Many people today are low in red blood cell and intercellular chromium. Chromium is necessary for proper metabolism of sugar, and is useful to people with diabetes and hypoglycemia. The average American eats too much sugar, which depletes the body of chromium. Lack of chromium can cause headaches, mood swings, fatigue and sweating.

Chromium is also essential in the manufacture of *trypsin*, a digestive enzyme which is necessary for the absorption of other nutrients. It is important too in the metabolizing of cholesterol. Proper levels of chromium prevent the accumulation of deposits on the arterial walls, thus reducing the risk of arteriosclerosis.

Studies on nutrition and the elderly show that about 70% of people over 70 are chromium deficient. In addition, 40% of people over 40 have abnormal glucose-tolerance test results, which suggest chromium deficiency. The most popular source of chromium today is *chromium picolinate*. This nutritional supplement has been shown to be useful in stabilizing blood sugar, increasing energy, and maintaining weight loss.

IRON

Iron is important to the left hemisphere of the brain (in right-handed people), and affects word fluency. For some reason not yet fully understood, low iron impairs thinking and word finding in women, but not in men.

One in ten premenopausal women is low in iron. Harold Hanstead at the University of Texas found that women given 30 mg of iron a day improved their scores on memory tests by 15 to 20%. Iron appears to improve verbal recall, the ability to repeat what you have heard.

Recently some studies have suggested that too much iron in the diet can increase the risk of heart attack in men.

MANGANESE

Manganese is important for normal central nervous system function. It is found in nuts, seeds, and whole grains, especially buckwheat. It has been demonstrated that like chromium, a manganese deficiency can lower your glucose tolerance, and contribute to a diabetic condition. Manganese is also involved in the metabolism of choline, which is discussed in the next chapter, and vitamin C.

SELENIUM

Selenium is one of the most poisonous substances known to man. It is also absolutely necessary for our survival. Selenium is a *trace element,* which means it is present in extremely small quantities in the body. As well as being an antioxidant, selenium increases the effectiveness of vitamin E, and has been shown to be an anticarcinogen.

Several studies show that selenium can reduce cancer in animals. Other studies suggest that there is a relationship between low selenium levels and heart attack. Selenium also helps remove toxic metals such as mercury and lead from the body.

Foods high in selenium include garlic, liver, brewer's yeast, brown rice, and eggs. It is also available in multivitamins and in tablet form, combined with vitamin E.

ZINC

Many older people do not get enough zinc in their diet because they can't afford the foods (such as meat and seafood) that contain it. Low zinc causes loss of taste and smell, which lessens appetite.

Mari Golub from U.C. Davis studied the effects of dietary zinc using Rhesus monkeys. One group was given one hundred parts per million and the other group four parts per million in their daily diet. The low zinc animals took three times longer to learn the difference between a circle and a cross. Other studies also suggest that zinc improves associative memory.

In a recent government hearing, reports were given indicating that thirty-two states now have zinc-deficient soil. This makes it possible that many of us are zinc deficient.

On the other hand, *too much* zinc can be dangerous. Some researchers believe that zinc can increase the amount of toxic amyloid (a protein that plays an important role in causing Alzheimer's) that is deposited in the brain. Investigators at Massachusetts General Hospital found that a increases in zinc caused the amyloid molecules to clump together within only two minutes.

Although the results were preliminary, there is enough evidence to warn against taking megadoses of zinc. In addition. dietary zinc has been shown to markedly decrease mental functioning in people with Alzheimer's. A safe dose of zinc is about 15 mg a day.

GERMANIUM

Germanium is found in minute quantities in many medicinal herbs, including garlic, ginseng and chlorella. Technically, germanium is a trace element found in the Earth's crust. Germainium has been considered as a memory enhancer since the 1980s. It increases the body's ability to accept oxygen and therefore increases brain function.

Research suggests that germanium stimulates the immune system and has a positive effect against tumors, cancer, and several viruses.

Germanium also has the ability to capture heavy metal toxins in your body and to remove them within twenty-four hours.

Some of the most common natural sources of germanium are garlic, onions, aloe vera, watercress, barley, the herbs comfrey, ginseng, angelica, and suma, and shiitake and reishi mushrooms. The recommended dosage is 30 mg daily, while some nutritionists recommend 60 mg per day.

CALCIUM

Over half of all Americans don't get enough calcium. Although it's well-known that calcium helps keep bones and teeth strong, it also plays a vital role in other body functions.

For example, as discussed previously, over 50 million Americans suffer from high blood pressure. Left untreated, even mildly elevated blood pressure can reduce the life expectancy of a 35-year-old by several years.

Studies suggest that in some people, increased calcium consumption can help control blood pressure without medication. The results of a thirteen-year survey by the National Center for Health Statistics showed that people who consumed 1300 mg of calcium per day were 12 % less likely to develop high blood pressure than those consuming 300 mg per day. Those under age 40 had a 25% reduction in risk. For this reason, it may be prudent for those with hypertension to increase their calcium intake.

Several studies suggest that calcium may also lower cholesterol. In a study at the Center for Human Nutrition at the University of Texas, three men with moderately high cholesterol levels were given a low calcium diet (410 mg. per day) for ten days. Then, for another ten days, the men were given 2,200 mg of calcium daily.

The results showed that the high-calcium levels reduced the level of total cholesterol by 6% and lowered LDL cholesterol (the bad cholesterol) by 11%, while HDL (good cholesterol) levels stayed the same.

CHAPTER TWENTY-THREE

NUTRIENTS THAT IMPROVE MEMORY

Proper nutrition is essential for a healthy mind. Vitamins and minerals are essential nutrients that have specific effects on brain function, but many nutrients that are not classified as vitamins or minerals also have substantial effects on memory.

PHENYLALANINE

Noradrenalin is a substance in the brain that is similar to adrenalin. It acts in the brain as a stimulant, and affects emotion, memory, and sex drive.

Noradrenalin seems to play an important role in learning and memory. In experiments with animals, learning has been prevented by administering drugs that rob the brain of noradrenalin.

Coffee is stimulating because caffeine increases the brain's sensitivity to noradrenalin. Coffee doesn't make noradrenalin, but raises its use. When the brain's supply of noradrenaline becomes depleted, coffee will no longer give you a lift, but instead will make you feel spaced out and jittery.

Like caffeine, other stimulants such as amphetamine, Ritalin, magnesium pemoline, and cocaine initially increase the amount of noradrenalin used by the brain, but these drugs interfere with the brain's ability to recycle the chemical, which results in a low level of the substance. Depression and memory problems are the result.

Noradrenalin is made from the amino acid *phenylalanine*. But consuming phenylalanine will not increase brain levels unless it is taken in along with carbohydrate, which helps it pass the blood-brain barrier.

For phenylalanine to be transformed into noradrenalin, supplements of vitamin B_6, folic acid, vitamin C, and copper are also required.

As the brain ages, the number of noradrenalin receptors decreases. Supplementing the brain with phenylalanine and the proper cofactors compensates for the loss. When used in this manner, phenylalanine can also act as an antidepressant.

RNA (Ribonucleic acid)

Studies show that high levels of brain RNA improve learning and memory. When *ribonuclease*, a substance that destroys RNA, is injected into the brains of animals, they are unable to learn. Several companies now manufacture RNA supplements.

L-GLUTAMINE

The brain uses this amino acid as a source of energy. It readily crosses the blood brain barrier, and has been shown to improve concentration. It has also been shown to reduce the craving for alcohol and sugar.

Zimmerman, Burgemiester, and Putnam used Glutamic acid on sixty nine mentally retarded children ages 5 to 17, whose average I.Q. was 65. For one year they were given twelve grams of glutamic acid per day in their diet. The average gain in I.Q. was 11 points, the highest gain was 17 points. Roger Williams raised I.Qs of retarded children with l-glutamine. This is fascinating evidence that we actually may be able to raise our I.Q. for nutritional modification.

TYROSINE

Tyrosine has shown to be an antidepressant. The brain uses tyrosine to make the neurotransmitters dopamine and norepinephrine, both of which play a part in thinking, long-term memory, and alertness. When tyrosine levels rise in the brain, they stimulate it to peak levels of clarity for several hours. Tyrosine is found in meat, poultry, seafood and beans, or can be taken as a nutritional supplement.

COENZYME Q_{10}

This enzyme acts as an antioxidant to retard brain aging. It has also been shown to increase cardiac strength, which helps brain blood flow.

Much of the research on brain function and CoQ_{10} has been done by Dr. Denham Harman of Omaha, Nebraska. Harmon was one of the pioneers in linking free radicals to the aging process. Harman formulated a theory linking Alzheimer's disease to free-radical damage, which causes mutations in DNA.

According to Harmon's theory, the DNA damage occurs early in life, possibly even during fetal development. But the effects of this damage are not seen until at least middle age.

The consequences include an accumulation of hydrogen peroxide and hydroxyl radicals, chemicals that Harman sees as having a role in the development of Alzheimer's disease. Harman believes that CoQ_{10} and other antioxidants can improve mental function, even in cases of Alzheimer's.

ACETYLCHOLINE

Acetylcholine is a neurotransmitter involved in transferring short-term memory to long term memory, acetylcholine also plays a role in movement, sleep, and such primitive drives as the desire for sex, food, and acquisition.

In an experiment where young people were given *scopolamine*, a drug which blocks the use of acetylcholine, the subjects showed a pattern of learning deficits which resemble the pattern found in old age. Several over-the-counter sleep aids, such as *Sleepeze,* contain scopolamine, and could therefore interfere with memory.

The amount of acetylcholine in the brain decreases with age. Since it has been well-established that acetylcholine plays an important part in memory, scientists have looked at ways to increase brain levels of this substance. There are several ways this can be accomplished, which will be discussed in the following section.

PHYSOSTIGMINE

Physostigmine is a drug extracted from a poisonous plant called the *calabar bean*. Researchers discovered in 1979 that the drug could improve memory in old Rhesus monkeys. Human studies, however failed to duplicate these memory gains. Recently it was discovered that the length of dosage is the critical factor. Yaakov Stern from Columbia University has found that humans who use the drug for at least six to eight months show memory improvement. Proper dosage must be established to minimize side effects. The drug's memory boosting power lies in its ability to prolong the activity of acetylcholine.

CHOLINE

Choline was discovered by Dr. A. Strecher in 1930. It is often classified as a B vitamin, but it's technically not a vitamin. Choline is used by the body to help build cells, to keep the liver from forming fatty deposits, and to manufacture *acetylcholine*, a neurotransmitter necessary for memory. Taking supplements of choline appears to increase the brain's ability to take in information. It increases attention span, and facilitates transfer of information from short-term to long-term memory.

In a study done at the National Institute of Mental Health (NIMH), subjects given a single ten-gram dose of choline showed improvement in both memory retention and recall. An effective dose of choline is 3,000 to 10,000mg.

Unfortunately, Alzheimer's patients given choline show little or no improvement. Studies of the brains of Alzheimer's patients reveal that they lack the important enzyme *choline -acetyltransferase*, which is needed to convert choline into acetylcholine.

LECITHIN

Lecithin is found in every living cell. Thirty percent of the brain is lecithin. High levels of lecithin compounds (such as *phosphatidylcholine* and *phosphatidyl-ethanolamine*) in the blood may have a protective effect against Alzheimer's disease.

In the blood stream, lecithin helps prevent cholesterol and fats from accumulating on the walls of the arteries. In the liver, lecithin metabolizes fat and lessens the chance of liver degeneration.

Lecithin supplementation stimulates the production of *acetylcholine*, the neurotransmitter necessary for the transfer of short-term memory to long-term memory. Taking choline does this also, but lecithin contains many other ingredients, such as fatty acids, sugars, and phosphate.

Choline metabolizes rapidly—blood levels peak within a few hours of taking it, but lecithin breaks down slowly, and provides the brain with a more constant supply of choline.

AL721 (Egg Lecithin)

AL721 is a type of lecithin that is extracted from egg yolk. The number 721 signifies that the compound is seven parts neutral lipids (which are oils), two parts phosphatydylcholine, and one part phosphatydylethanolamine. AL721 is used in Israel to treat viral diseases, senility, and AIDS. Research suggests that the compound enhances a cell's ability to repair cell membranes. This product is available in the United States under the brand name *Eggs-ACT*.

ACETYL-L-CARNITINE

Research scientist Luciano Angellucci, M.D., who studied aging and the brain for many years, discovered a substance called *acetyl-l-carnitine* (ALC) which is found in muscle tissue, and converts fat into energy.

Acetyl-l-carnitine is similar to another form of the amino acid called *carnitine. However*, Angellucci says taking carnitine alone will not work for older people, because the enzymes needed to transform it into acetyl-l-carnitine decrease with age.

Studies show that ALC slows the loss of *nerve growth factor* (NGF), a group of chemicals that helps brain cells stay young. These important chemicals provide support for the healthy functioning of brain cells, especially in the hippocampus and frontal cortex of the brain.

The degenerative changes associated with brain aging seem to be caused, in part, by a decline in Nerve Growth Factor. Several studies show that supplementing NGF reverses both physical and behavioral deficits in aged rats. Giving the rats ALC increased the NGF levels by 39% in the central nervous system.

ALC also increases the level of an enzyme that scavenges free radicals, and it enhances the function of an important neurotransmitter, *acetylcholine,* which plays an essential role in learning and memory.

Long-term treatment with ALC completely prevented the loss of *choline acetyltransferase* (CHAT) activity in the brains of rats. CHAT is the enzyme that helps to transform choline into acetylcholine.

The nutrient ALC also appears to slow the progression of Alzheimer's disease. In Milan, Italy, 130 patients with Alzheimer's Disease were given 2 grams a day of ALC for a year, and were compared to patients receiving placebos. The results showed a markedly slower rate of deterioration in patients receiving acetyl-l-carnitine. In another study the nutrient was successful in slowing the cognitive decline of sixty-three people diagnosed with Alzheimer's. These patients scored higher than untreated individuals in thirteen of fourteen measures of mental performance.

At Columbus University, people with Alzheimer's who were given 2,500 to 3,500mg of acetyl-l-carnitine per day showed significantly less memory deterioration than those given a placebo. Studies in England and at Georgia State University show similar results.

New research shows that brain cell aging can indeed be slowed or prevented by treatment with acetyl-l-carnitine. In a recent study done in Rome, scientists used ALC to prevent the age-dependent loss of neurons in certain areas of the rat brain, especially the hippocampus. In another study, rats treated for eight months with ALC showed no age-related loss of ability to find their way through a maze.

ALC appears to have both curative and preventive properties when given to elderly people. ALC might be even more beneficial in slowing or preventing cognitive and behavioral deficits in normally-aging persons without overt signs of disease. The evidence suggests that long-term treatment with acetyl -l-carnitine could stop the progress of age-related neurodegenerative diseases such as Alzheimer's Disease and could slow normal aging in humans.

New research suggests that acetyl-l-carnitine repairs this DNA damage in peripheral blood lymphocytes (white blood cells), suggesting that it can help prevent the age-related decline of the immune system. DNA is constantly under attack from environmental toxins, and radiation, and these attacks cause structural damage to the DNA molecule.

This nutrient is available in the United States at health food stores, and from Cardiovascular Research, Ltd. 1061-B Shary Circle, Concord, CA 94518 (800) 888-4585. Sigma Tau Pharmaceuticals in Gaithsburg, MD, is the American developer of the nutrient.

NADH

Nicotinamide-adenine-dinucleotide (NADH) is a co-enzymatic form of vitamin B_3. Although as of this writing there has been only one published report about this nutrient, it does show promise in reducing the symptoms of Alzheimer's disease. In the study, there was an improvement in metal function within twelve weeks, using 5 mg per day. This substance is now available in health food stores.

ARGININE

Arginine is an amino acid produced naturally in the human body. It can also be found in small amounts in many nuts and seeds. Recent studies show that arginine can lower blood pressure, enhance the immune system, and stimulate the release of human growth hormone. In animal studies, arginine speeds up wound healing and reduces the damage caused by heart attacks and strokes.

The body converts arginine to *spermine*, which is a chemical found in semen, blood tissue, and brain cells. If you are low in spermine, you may start to show early signs of memory loss and senility.

A 1990 headline in *The New York Times* declared: "Human Growth Hormone Reverses the Effects of Aging." This synthetically produced growth hormone costs $20,000 a year to take, which put it out of reach. But two progressive nutritionists developed a much cheaper, but equally effective alternative.

Durk Pearson and Sandy Shaw, authors of the best-selling book *Life Extension*, came up with an alternative way to increase the levels of growth hormones in the brain. They recommend combining six grams of arginine, 600mg of choline, and 500 mg vitamin B_5.

Studies with human subjects show that arginine combats cancer and cardiovascular disease. A 1991 study in Germany showed that arginine supplementation increased the blood flow in the small blood vessels of the human heart by as much as

198%. The researchers feel that arginine does this by restoring the function of endothelial cells that line the walls of the blood vessels. Arginine is available in health food stores everywhere.

TRYPTOPHAN

The amino acid, tryptophan is used by your brain to make the neurotransmitter serotonin, a substance which induces sleep and slows down overall nerve transmission and reaction time. High levels of serotonin are needed to ward off depression. *Prozac*, the most popular antidepressant in history, works by raising levels of serotonin in the brain.

Tryptophan is found in milk, dairy products, bananas, sunflower seeds, and turkey. Tryptophan used to be available as a supplement, and was used to treat depression and insomnia, but a contaminant found in one batch of it caused the FDA to take all tryptophan off the market.

After a meal containing both protein and carbohydrate, if tryptophan crosses the blood-brain barrier before tyrosine can, you will become sleepy. For this reason, eat protein before you eat the carbohydrates in your meal if you wish to stay awake and alert.

OMEGA-3 FATTY ACIDS

An important group of fatty acids, called *omega-3s*, is found in high levels in cold-water fish, such as salmon. The fish highest in omega-3 fatty acids are mackerel, salmon, bluefish, tuna, Atlantic sturgeon, sablefish, herring, anchovies, sardines, and lake trout. Another potent source of this substance is flax-seed oil.

Omega-3 oils have the ability to block disease processes at the cellular level. In addition, they are very important in preventing cardiovascular disease, stroke and heart attacks.

PROTEIN

The need for protein depends on many factors, including age, body weight, general health, and level of mental exertion.

Most nutritionists believe that, on the whole, Americans eat too much protein. For many years, red meat consumption has been the hallmark of the American diet. But red meat has been linked to many diseases and health conditions such as arteriosclerosis, and the trend has been to reduce red meat consumption.

However, many vegetarians and many older people do not get enough protein in their diet. Vegetarians sometimes simply eliminate protein and do not replace it by eating the right combinations of beans, seeds, and nuts. As a result they are chronically protein deficient, and often fatigued, confused, and unmotivated.

Many older people simply cannot afford enough protein to stay healthy and are therefore perpetually malnourished. Proper protein is essential for peak mental performance.

SHELLFISH

Shellfish such as oysters and clams are very low in carbohydrates and fat, and are very high in protein. Eating 3 or 4 ounces of shellfish as an appetizer delivers an adequate dose of tyrosine quickly to the brain. For this reason shellfish can stimulate mental activity, improve mood, and elevate brain performance. Be aware that shellfish tend to accumulate more toxins and pollutants than regular fish, because they filter their nutrients from sea water.

CHAPTER TWENTY-FOUR

HERBS THAT
IMPROVE MEMORY

Millions of years before the age of medicine, humankind was using herbs to heal their woes and soothe their pains. All over the world, people have discovered the magic healing powers of plants. The modern sciences of medicine and pharmacology are in fact outgrowths of herbology. Many modern medicines actually are derived from herbs. For example, aspirin, one of the most widely used drugs in the world, is an extract of willow bark.

For many centuries, various flowers, herbs, and roots have been used for the improvement of memory. Science has verified that some of these plants do indeed have positive effects.

Although herbs are natural substances and relatively safe, do not take any herb without consulting a professional herbalist. Before you take any of these herbs, tell your doctor what you intend to do, as herbs can be powerful, and may interact with other medication you are taking.

GINKGO BILOBA

The first written record of the use of ginkgo appears in a Chinese medical text written in 2800 B.C. Ginkgo biloba is an extract of the leaf of the ginkgo tree. A native of China, this amazing tree lives for more than 1,000 years.

In 1754, the tree was introduced to England. Since that time, hundreds of studies have revealed that this ancient herb has the power to improve memory, clarify concentration, and aid in emotional stability.

There are over seventy-five published papers documenting the ability of ginkgo to improve and protect vascular health and to enhance mental function. Currently, ginkgo is the most frequently prescribed drug in Europe because of its numerous disease preventing properties.

Ginkgo has also been shown to have a positive effect on asthma, allergies, and blood clots. The gingko extract also aids brain function by acting as a free radical scavenger, and by increasing the brain's ability to use oxygen. Ginkgo extract is available in most health food stores. It is made in both oral and injectable forms.

GOTO-KOLA

This herb, whose botanical name is *Centella asiatica*, originates in India, where it grows along stone walls and rocky outcroppings. Ayurvedic practitioners use Gotu-kola to combat aging and senility. This herb has been used for centuries as a memory aid. Gotu-kola is also found in Asia and Australia, where it is used to heal wounds, improve skin, and reduce cellulite. It is also used there as a brain tonic to improve memory and increase intelligence.

In a recent study done with thirty developmentally disabled children, a twelve week program of Gotu-kola supplementation improved attentiveness and concentration. The active ingredients in Goto-kola are thought to be a group of substances called *triterpenes*.

In India, people take Gotu-kola to increase mental stamina and memory. The recommended dosage is one cup of tea at bedtime.

KOLA

Kola originates from Africa. Its main action is as a central nervous system stimulant, increasing alertness.

SCHIZANDRA

Schizandra is an herb that originates from China. This is also a central nervous system stimulant, and an *adaptogen*, a substance that helps that body maintain metabolic balance.

CARROT JUICE

Carrot juice is a long-standing natural treatent for mental illness, including schizophrenia. It contains high levels of beta-carotene. Although this is a popular tonic for nerve problems, beyond its vitamin content, there is little hard scientific evidence for its effectiveness.

HOLLY

For many generations, holly seeds have been said to strengthen memory. I could find no scientific studies to substantiate this.

VALERIAN ROOT

Valerian root, from the family *valerianaceae*, has been used as a medicinal herb for several thousand years. It was taken by the ancient Greeks as a digestive aid, and for urinary tract problems. The herb was also used by the Chinese and in Indian Ayurvedic medicine. It is popular today throughout Europe, Canada, Mexico, and New Zealand.

The valerian plant is a perennial herb that grows up to five feet high from a short rhizome. The plant has small pink, lavender, or sometimes red flowers. Although many types of valerian have been use medicinally, the wild root is usually stronger than the plants found in the garden. The species used most often is *Valeriana officinalis*.

The name valerian comes from the Latin *valere* which means "to be in health." Most people dislike the smell of valerian, but researchers believe that the same chemicals that give the herb its odor are responsible for its medicinal properties.

Most modern herbalists recommend valerian for its sedative qualities. Valerian root is a natural tranquilizer and sleep inducer. The few scientific studies that have been done on valerian show it to be an effective sedative, and that it improves the quality of sleep. Good sleep means improved memory.

Valerian is non-toxic, nonaddictive, and has very few side effects. Valerian may cause increased urination in some people.

GINSENG

Ginseng is of Chinese origin. Its beneficial effects on the human body have been known to the Chinese for at least 4,000 years. It is quite possibly the most widely used medicinal herb in the

Orient. It has been used for centuries by the Russians and Chinese to increase stamina and alertness

Ginseng is also an adaptogenic herb. This means it is an herb that helps to bring your body back to equilibrium. Sometimes ginseng is taken as a tincture, a liquid solution which combines an extract of the herb with alcohol.

The ginseng root, which is the part of the plant used to make the tincture, resembles a tiny human. This is why the ancient healers called ginseng the "root of life plant." Around 200 A.D., a Chinese emperor dubbed it *panax ginseng*, meaning "panacea from ginseng," and the botanical name has remained with the plant ever since.

Ginseng contains a family of chemicals called *saponins* (also called *glycosides* or *ginsenosides*), which influence the metabolism of certain brain chemicals involved in mental functions.

Ginseng improves mental performance, especially in conditions of stress, fatigue, and overwork by increasing the levels of the neurotransmitter *norepinephrine,* which increases arousal and attention. Stress can deplete the brain's supply of norepinephrine, but ginseng levels out its release and inhibits its depletion.

Ginseng comes in the form of tinctures, pills, extracts, capsules, tablets, powders, pastes, as dried roots, granulated teas, and even as an element in wines and liquors. But typically you will find it as an extract.

Doses of 500 to 3,000mg of the tincture per day are recommended. It is suggested that you start with the low dose and gradually increase it. Like ginkgo, its effects are cumulative. The herb should be taken for a month before seeing major effects

CALAMUS ROOT

This herb, also called *Sweet Flag,* is sometimes used to treat epilepsy, to strengthen the memory, and to stimulate higher brain functions.

Ayurvedic practitioners feel that the herb has *sattvic energy,* which pertains to clarity of consciousness. Many Ayurvedic healers consider calamus to be one of the most effective herbs for mental clarity. They have praised calamus for centuries for its ability to purify and revitalize the brain, increase blood circulation, strengthen memory, and stimulate awareness.

Herbalists recommend a pinch of powdered calamus (250 -500 mg) mixed with ¼ to ½ teaspoon of honey in the morning and in the evening.

NUTMEG

Nutmeg is considered to be a tonic for both the heart and brain. When taken in quantities no greater than a pinch at a time, it is also a relaxant which can help eliminate insomnia and increase restful sleep. Large amounts of this herb can be toxic.

A chemical called *thujione* which is related to the nutmeg family is also a powerful brain stimulant. It is found in small amounts in vermouth, and is a component of cedar leaf oil.

BASIL

When taken as a powder in doses of 250 mg to 1 gm or as a tea mixed with honey, basil is said to heighten the acuteness of the senses, strengthen nerve tissue, increase memory, and promote clarity of thought.

BHRINGARAJ

This Ayurvedic herb also grows in the American Southwest. It has also been called *fesharaia*, or *Eclipta*, (which literally means "ruler of the hair" because it is claimed to promote hair growth). This herb is used to calm the mind, to promote restful sleep, and to act as a general brain tonic.

LEMON BALM

Lemon balm, also called *Melissa officinalis*, has been used for centuries as a memory tonic. Seventeenth Century herbalist John Evelyn wrote, "Balm is sovereign for the brain, strengthening the memory and powerfully chasing away melancholy." The recommended dosage is several cups per day, a few hours apart.

SAGE

Sage is recognized in Ayurvedic medicine and in traditional Chinese medicine for its ability to reduce the severity of emotional upsets and to promote calmness. Sage is sometimes mixed with Gotu-kola or Bhringaraj.

HARITAKI

Haritaki (also called *Chebulic myrobalan*, and *Terminalia chebula)* is a fruit that is known as the "king of medicines" in Tibet. It is said to rejuvenate and energize the brain and nerves. Haritaki is available as a decoction. powder, or paste. Decoctions may be made by boiling the herb in water.

KELP

Kelp is a nutritionally rich sea vegetable that also has tension-reducing properties. Kelp may achieve this effect by insulating heart and nerve tissue from stress. It is also high in iodine, which is essential for proper thyroid function.

PEPPERMINT

Peppermint is believed by many herbalists to prevent congestion in cerebral blood circulation. It is also widely used as a tonic to calm jangled nerves. Peppermint is said to increase concentration. Students using peppermint before exams have scored better on tests, because of the stimulating effect it has on olfactory memory.

SKULLCAP

Skullcap (*Scutellaria lateriflora*) is a commonly used nerve tonic, which is also useful in treating insomnia. It is said to have a positive effect on mental clarity which may be due to its ability to reduce nervous tension.

WOOD BETONY

Officially called *Betonica officianalis*, wood betony is known to reduce tension and nervousness, and is used by herbalists as a sedative.

ROSEMARY

Rosemary (*Rosemarinus officinalus*) has been known for centuries as the "herb of memory." It was believed by the ancient

Greeks that putting a stalk of rosemary in one's hair would improve memory. It's also been used by Chinese practitioners to treat circulatory problems, and as a smooth muscle stimulant.

ALLIUM SATIVUM

Allium Sativum is an herb used for centuries for the treatment of circulatory problems. This substance prevents blood clots and protects against stroke, atherosclerosis, and heart attacks. It appears to lower LDL and raise HDL. A study at Loma Linda University showed that taking *allium sativum* resulted in a 12 to 31% drop in cholesterol levels.

EUROPEAN BILBERRY

Bilberry extract strengthens the walls of capillaries, which are tiny blood vessels. Weak capillaries are a major cause of transient ischemic attacks (TIAs) which are discussed in chapter 12 of this book. Bilberry extract protects brain capillaries against high blood pressure. The extract also reduces the risk of brain hemorrhage induced by hypertension. Bilberry also reduces the blood clots by inhibiting platelet aggregation.

Another benefit of bilberry extract is its effects on night vision. During World War II, British pilots reported a dramatic increase in night vision after consuming bilberry jam. An Italian study recently showed that 75% of people improve their night vision after taking bilberry supplements.

ST. JOHN'S WORT

Hypericum perforatum is a native plant of Europe, West Asia, North Africa, Madeira, and the Azores. Today it can also be found in North America and Australia.

Known in the U.S. as *St. John's Wort*, this herb has a long medicinal history. It can be traced back to the ancient Greeks and Romans, who used the plant to treat burns, ulcers, malaria, kidney ailments, and nervous disorders. *Hypericum perforatum* has for many centuries been used as a folk remedy for depression, anxiety, mania, hysteria, and insomnia.

Today, however, Hypericum is used as a natural alternative to prescription antidepressants. Over twenty-five controlled studies on Hypericum have been published which show that it works as well as antidepressant drugs with fewer side effects. In a German study, fifteen women suffering from depression were given hypericum and reported substantial improvement in their quality of life. This was measured by a greater interest in life, improved feelings of self-worth, increased appetite, and more normal sleep patterns. In another study, 60% of those taking a Hypericum extract reported good to very good results compared with 10% in the placebo group.

The active ingredient in the herb is *hypericin* which has the ability to inhibit the activity of monoamine oxidase (MAO), the enzyme linked to depression. The most common side effect of hypericum is upset stomach, which can be avoided by taking it with food. The dosage needs to be sufficient for the desired results to be obtained. Although the effective dose may vary with each individual, up to 900 mg a day can be taken safely.

For more information about herbs, contact The Herb Research Foundation, 1007 Pearl Street, Suite 200, Boulder CO 80302, (303) 449-2265; or The American Botanical Council, PO Box 201660, Austin TX 78720, (512) 331-8868.

GLOSSARY

Age Associated Memory Impairment (AAMI)   A gradual decline in several components of memory that comes with age. With AAMI, memory retrieval takes longer and new skills are learned more slowly. The National Institute of Mental Health first defined and recognized AAMI in 1986. About 20% of Americans over 50 suffer from this condition.

Acetylcholine   A neurotransmitter that is found in the *hippocampus*, and is necessary for proper memory function.

Alzheimer's Disease   The most common type of *senile dementia*. This disease is characterized by memory loss, and the presence of *neuritic plaques* and *neurofibrillary* tangles in the brain.

Amnesia   The loss of ability to learn, store or remember information

Anoxia   A lack of oxygen to the brain. This lack can kill brain cells within three minutes. The drug Hydergine is said to lessen the effects of anoxia.

Autobiographical Memory   The memory of one's personal past. Studies show that this type of memory is often very inaccurate.

Cerebral Cortex The outer layer of the brain, which is responsible for higher mental functioning.

Cognition Any brain process related to thinking or reasoning.

Cognitive Relating to or being conscious mental activity, such as thinking, remembering, learning and using language skills.

Confabulation The act of constructing false memories, often to cover up memory loss. This behavior is associated with Korsakoff's psychosis, a condition caused by chronic alcoholism.

Dementia Any condition that impairs *cognitive* function.

Hippocampus A small bundle of nerve cells found in both sides of the brain that are necessary for memory storage.

Infantile Amnesia The inability to recall the first few years of life. Most people can remember very little before the age of three.

Lipofuscin The accumulation of debris within a cell. This is what causes age spots. The accumulation of lipofuscin in the brain is thought to cause cognitive problems.

Long-Term Memory The type of memory that stores information permanently.

Mnemonics Any memory improvement technique that involves visualization, association, or the linking together of data. The word comes from the Greek Goddess *Mnemosyne*, the goddess of memory.

Multi-Infarct Dementia The second most common cause of

dementia, following Alzheimer's disease which is number one. This condition is brought on by a series of tiny strokes. Untreated high blood pressure is usually a contributing cause.

Neuritic Plaque   An accumulation of degenerated nerve cell material and debris.

Neurofibrillary Tangle   An accumulation of abnormal fibers, tangled inside the interior of a brain cell. These tangles are fond most frequently in the part of the brain called the hippo-campus, which is responsible fort transferring short term memory to long term memory.

Neuron   A nerve cell. The neuron is responsible for information processing in the brain.

Neurotransmitters   A class of chemicals found in the brain that transmit signals from one neuron to another. There are thought to be about 200 types of neurotransmitters.

Smart Drugs   A class of drugs, also known as *nootropics,* which improve memory in normal, healthy people as well as those with memory problems.

Senile Dementia   A group of disorders that cause memory loss and other cognitive problems. Alzheimer disease is the most common form of senile dementia.

Short-Term Memory   The initial storage of information. Short term memory lasts about fifteen seconds, and can store about one phone number. Most memory problems involve the failure of information to travel from short-term to long-term memory.

Transient Global Amnesia   The temporary inability to recall any biographical information. This usually occurs as a result of a blow to the head, and lasts from a few minutes to a few hours.

REFERENCES

CHAPTER 1: MEMORY LOSS

Crook, T., Bartus, R., Ferris, S., Whitehouse, P., Cohen, G., and Gershon, S. (1986) Age-associated memory impairment: proposed diagnostic criteria and measures of clinical change—Report of a National Institute of Mental Health Workgroup. *Developmental Neuropsychology* 2(4): 261-276.

Crook, T. & Larrabee, G. (1988) Age-associated memory impairment: diagnostic criteria and treatment strategies. *Psychopharmacology Bulletin* 24(4): 509-514.

Noll, R. & Turkington, C. (1994) *The Encyclopedia of Memory and Memory Disorders*. Facts on File, NY, p5.

Birren J. (1977) *Handbook of the Psychology of Aging* Van Nostrand Rhinehold, NY.

Birren, J. & Cunningham, W (1983) Psychology of Adult Development and Aging *Annual Review of Psychology* 34:543-575.

Buell, S. (1981) New thoughts on old neurons *Seminars in Neurology* 1(1):31-35.

Jarvik, L. (1975) The aging nervous system: Clinical aspects. *Aging* 1.

Marwick, C. (1993) What is age-associated memory impairment? *JAMA, The Journal of the American Medical Association* 269 (1):356.

Gilbert, J. (1971) Patterns of declining memory. *Journal of Gerontology* 28(1).

Katzman, R & Terry, R (1983) The Neurology of Aging F.A. Davis Company, Philadelphia.

Racagni, G. & Mendlewicz, J. (1992) *Treatment of Age Related Cognitive Dysfunction: Pharmacological and Clinical Evaluation* Karger, Basil.

Wilson B. & Moffat, N. (1984) *Clinical Management of Memory Problems.* Croom Helm, London.

Poon, W. (1985) Differences in human memory with aging: nature, causes, and clinical applications, in the *Handbook of the Psychology of Aging*, 2nd ed., J. E. Birren and K.W. Schaie, eds. Van Nostrand Reinhold, NY. pp427-62.

Gutfeld, G., et al. (1991) The memory remains: Recall ability may not fade with age. *Prevention* 43(2):18.

Roberts, P. (1983) Memory strategy instruction with the elderly: What should memory training be the training of? in *Cognitive Strategy Research: Psychological Foundations*, M. Pressley and J. Levin, eds. Springer-Verlag, NY pp75-100.

Willis.S.& Schaie, K. (1986) Practical Intelligence in Later Adulthood, in *Practical Intelligence: Nature and Origins of Competence in the Everyday World*, R. Sternberg and R. Wagner, eds. Cambridge University Press, Cambridge, pp236-68.

Poon, L., Walsh-Sweeney, L., and Fozard, L. (1980) Memory Skill Training for the Elderly: Salient Issues on the Use of Imagery Mnemonics," in *New Directions in Memory and Aging*, Poon, L., Fozard, J., Cermak,, L., Arenberg, D., and Thompson, L. Erlbaum,, eds. Hillsdale NJ. Pp461-84;

McEvoy, C.,& Moon, J. (1988) Assessment and Treatment of Everyday Memory Problems in the Elderly, in *Practical Aspects of Memory: Current Research and Issues*, M. Gruneberg,, P. Morris, and R. Sykes, eds. Wiley, Chichester, England

Youngjohn, J., & Crook, T., (1993) Stability of everyday memory in age-associated memory impairment: A longitudinal study. *Neuropsychology* v7 (n3):406-416.

Youngjohn, J., Larrabee, G., Crook, T. (1992) Discriminating age-associated memory impairment from Alzheimer's disease. *Psychological Assessment* 4 (1):54-59.

Golomb, J.; de Leon, M., et al. (1993) Hippocampal atrophy in normal aging. An association with recent memory impairment. *Archives of Neurology* 50(9):967-73.

CHAPTER 2: THE MANY TYPES OF MEMORY

Schab, F., & Crowder, R. eds. (1995) *Memory for Odors* Lawrence Erlbaum Associates, Inc, Mahwah, NJ.

Noll, R. & Turkington, C. (1994) Encyclopedia of Memory and Memory Disorders, p147. Facts on File

Engen, T. (1980) Why the aroma lingers on *Psychology Today*, May.

Wippich, W. (1990) Recall of odors: naming and autobiographical memories illustrate odor aftereffects. *Zeitschrift fur Experimentelle und Angewandte Psychologie* 37(4):679-95.

Winograd, E. (1980) Face Saving Memory *Psychology Today*, Feb.

Strobel, G. (1993) Different memories go different places *Science News* Nov 27. 44(1):367.

Baddely, A. (1986) *Working Memory* Oxford University Press, London.

Huyge, P. (1985) Voices, glances, flashbacks: our first memories: considering the novelty and richness of the first few years of life, why are our early memories so fragmented? *Psychology Today* Sept. p48(5).

CHAPTER 3: THE MEMORY PROCESS

Benderly, B. (1981) Flashbulb memory *Psychology Today*, June

Bower, G. (1961) Mood & Memory *Psychology Today* June

Lisman, J. & Marco, A.(1995) Storage of 7 +or - Short-term memories in oscillatory subcycles. *Science* 267(4):512.

CHAPTER 4: WHY WE FORGET

Baddeley, A. (1982) *Your Memory: A User's Guide*. Macmillan Publishing, NY.

Rappoport, D. (1961) *Emotions and Memory*. Science Editions Inc., NY.

Bornstein, A. (1983) Stress: A good memory's worst enemy *Exec - utive Fitness Newsletter*, vol 14(18).

Pressman, M.(1969) The cognitive function of the ego in psycho-analysis, II. Repression, incognizance and insight formation. *International Journal of Psychoanalysis* 50(3):343-51.

Colsher, P. & Wallace, R. (1990) Are hearing and visual dysfunction associated with cognitive impairment? A population- based approach. *Journal of Applied Gerontology* 9 (1):91-105.

CHAPTER 5: DEMENTIA

Buell, S. & Coleman, P. (1979) Dendritic growth in the aged human brain and failure of growth in senile dementia *Science* 206:854-856.

Rossor, M., Newman, S., et al. (1993) Alzheimer's disease in families with amyloid precursor protein mutations. *Annals of the New York Academy of Sciences*, 695:198-202.

Petersen. R., et al. (1995) Apolipoprotein E status as a predictor of the development of Alzheimer's disease in memory-impaired individuals. *JAMA, The Journal of the American Medical Association* 273 (5):274

(1992) Graphic Errors *Archives of Neurology* 49(11):1151-1156.

(1992) Weight Loss *International Psychogeriatrics* S4(1):103-118.

(1988) Nutrition *International Journal for Vitamin and Nutirition Research* 58(4): 462 465.

(1992) Aluminum & Magnesium *Magnesium Research* 5(1): 61-67.

CHAPTER 6: HOW TO STUDY

Hill, R., Storandt, M., Simeone, C. (1990) The Effect of Memory Skills Training and Incentives on Free Recall in Older Learners *Gerontology* 45(6):227-232.

Maddox, H. (1964) *How to Study* Crest Books, London.

Lorayne, H. (1976) *Good Memory, Successful Student.* Stein and Day, NY.

CHAPTER 7: HOW TO STOP LOSING AND FORGETTING THINGS

Cassedy, E. (1990) It isn't lost; I just can't find it: 6 easy ways to stop losing things *Woman's Day* Oct 2, 53(3):40.

Schreiner, S. Jr. (1988) How not to lose things. *Reader's Digest,* Sept 133(4):55.

CHAPTER 8: FACTORS FOR MAXIMIZING MEMORY

Roth, D (1948) *The Roth Memory Course.* Ralston Publishing, Cleveland, OH.

CHAPTER 9: MEMORY SYSTEMS

Grady, C., et al. (1995) Age-related reductions in human recognition memory due to impaired encoding. *Science* 269(4):218.

Giordano, G. (1982) Mnemonic techniques that improve reading comprehension *Clearing House* 56(1):164.

Yesavage, J. (1988) Techniques for cognitive training of memory in Age-Associated Memory Impairment. Symposium: Memory and aging. *Archives of Gerontology & Geriatrics,* Suppl, v1:185 -190.

CHAPTER 10: BIOLOGICAL RHYTHM AND MEMORY

Rubin, Z. (1979) Seasonal Rhythms in Behavior *Psychology Today,* Dec.

Folkard (1982) Circadian rhythms and human memory In F. Brown and R. Graeber, eds. *Rhythmic aspects of human behavior.* Erlbaum Associates, Hillsdale NJ, p313-344

Kripke (1982) Ultradian Rhythms in behavior and physiology. in F. Brown and R. Graeber, eds, *Rhythmic aspects of human behavior.* Erlbaum Associates, Hillsdale NJ.

Rasmunsen (1986) Physiological interactions of the basic rest-activity cycle of the brain *Psychoneuroendocrinology* 11(4) 389-405.

Chase, M. (1979) Every 90 Minutes a Brainstorm *Psychology Today* Nov.

CHAPTER 11: SLEEP, DREAMING, AND MEMORY

Palombo, S. (1978) *Dreaming and Memory.* Basic Books, NY.

Roffwarg, H., et al. (1978) The effects of sustained alterations of waking visual input on dream content. In *The Mind in Sleep: Psychology and Psychophysiology* Arkin, Antrobus, and Ellman, eds. Lawrence Erlbaum. Hillsdale NJ. p295.

Lichstein, M. (1990) Low sleep need causes confusion. *Brain/Mind Bulletin* 15(7). Originally in *Behavior Therapy* 19: 625-632

Hoddes, E. (1977) Does Sleep Help You Study? *Psychology Today,* April.

CHAPTER 12: BRAIN FUNCTION AND BLOOD FLOW

Reivich, M., et al. (1961) Reversal of blood flow through the vertebral artery and its effect on cerebral circulation. *New England Journal of Medicine* 263:878-885.

Sammartini, W. & O' Toole, J. (1964) Reversed vertebral artery flow: the effect of excercise. *Archives of Neurology* 10:590-594.

Jennett, B. et al (1976) Effect of Carotid Artery Surgery on Cerebral Blood Flow Excerpta Medica, Amsterdam.

Sangiorgio, M,. et al. (1992) Aerobic memory. (exercise and memory) *Prevention* 44(2):4

American Heart Association's Conference on Cardiovascular Disease Epidemiology and Prevention, March, 1996.

American Journal of Epidemiology, March, 1996

Medicine and Science in Sports and exercise, vol 10, 1978.

American Psychologist vol 36(4).

Foresman, L. & Lindbland, L (1983) *Psychosomatic Medicine.*

Runte, T. (1980) The bright stuff *Wholemind Newsletter* 1(12)

Haffner, S, et al. (1985) Coffee Consumption, Diet and Lipids. *American Journal of Epidemiology* 122:1-12.

Curb, J., et al. (1986) Coffee, caffeine and serum cholesterol in Japanese men in Hawaii. *American Journal of Epidemiology*123:648-655.

Mathias, S., et al. (1985) Coffee, plasma cholesterol, and lipoproteins: A population study in an adult community *American Journal of Epidemiology* 121:890-905.

Klatsky, A., et al. (1985) Coffee, tea and cholesterol. *American Journal of Cardiology* 55:577-578.

Thelle, D, et al. (1983) The Tromso Heart Study: Does coffee raise serum cholesterol?" *New England Journal of Medicine* 308:1454-1457.

Williams, P, et al. (1985) Coffee Intake and elevated cholesterol and apolipoprotein B Levels in Men." *JAMA* 253:1407-1411.

Coffee Consumption Linked with Rising Serum Cholesterol. Medical World News 26(15):2324, Aug. 12, 1985.

Forde, O. et al. (1985) The Tromso Heart Study: Coffee consumption and serum lipid concentrations in men with hypercholesterolaemia: A Randomised Intervention Study. *British Med J.* 290: 893-895.

Naismith, D. et al. (1970) The effect in volunteers of coffee and decaffein ated coffee on blood glucose, insulin, plasma lipids, and some factors involved in blood clotting. *Nutr. Metab.* 12:144-151.

Little, J., et al.(1966) Coffee and Serum Lipids in Coronary Heart Disease. *The Lancet* 1:732-734.

Kark, J., et al. (1985) Coffee, tea, and plasma cholesterol: The Jerusalem Lipid Research Clinic. *Br. Med J.* 292:699-704.

Haffner, S., et al. (1985) Coffee consumption, diet, and lipids." *Am. J. Epidemiol.* 122:1-12.

CHAPTER 13: BLOOD PRESSURE

Somomen, S., et al. (1983) Impairment of memory function by hypertensive medication *Archives of General Psychiatry* 40:1109-1112.

Ghosh, S. (1976) Methyldopa and Forgetfulness *The Lancet* 1:202-203.

Cahn, J. & Borzeix, M. (1983) Aging and hypertension as risk factors for the brain related to free radical damages to membranes. *Aging* 23:413-425.

Douglas, M., et al (1985) Effects of a raw food diet on hypertension and obesity. *Southern Medical Journal* 78(8):841.

Fioravanti, M., Agazzani, D; et al. (1991) Relationship between hypertension and early indicators of cognitive decline. *Dementia* 2(1):51-56.

Elias, M., Wolf, P., D'Agostino, R., Cobb, J., White, L., (1993) Untreated blood pressure level is inversely related to cognitive functioning: the Framingham Study. *American Journal of Epidemiology* 138(6):353-64.

Farmer, M., Kittner, S. et al. (1990) Longitudinally measured blood pressure, antihypertensive medication use, and cognitive performance: the Framingham Study. *Journal of Clinical Epidemiology* 43(5): 475 -80.

Steunberg G. (1991) Cough Syrup and Stroke *Longevity*, May

Madden, D. & Blumenthal, D. (No date)   *Health Psychology* 8:131-142.

CHAPTER 14: A WHACK ON THE HEAD

Kra, S. (1986) Subdural hematomas, in *Aging Myths*, p202.

Robinson R. (1984) Chronic subdural hematoma: surgical management in 133 patients. *Journal of Neurosurgery* 61(2):263-8.

Tsuboi K., Maki, Y., Nose, T., Matsuki, T. (1984) Psychiatric symptoms of patients with chronic subdural hematoma. *Neurological Surgery* 12(3 Suppl):275-9.

Rimel R., Giordani B., Barth J., Jane J. (1982) Moderate head injury: completing the clinical spectrum of brain trauma. *Neurosurgery* 11(3):344-51.

CHAPTER 15: DEPRESSION AND MEMORY

Kra, S. (1986) *Aging Myths: Reversible Causes of Mind and Memory Loss* McGraw-Hill, NY, p51.

Sabelli, H (1996) *J. Neuropsychiatry Clin. Neuroscience* 8:168-171.

Croog, S., et al. (1986) The Effects of Antihypertensive Therapy on the Quality of Life, *New England Journal of Medicine* 314:165-1664, 1986.

CHAPTER 16: HORMONES THAT AFFECT MEMORY

McGaugh, J. (1983) Preserving the presence of the past: Hormonal influences on memory storage *American Psychologist* 38(2) 161-173.

McGaugh, J. (1983) Hormonal influences on memory *Annual review of Psychology* 34: 297-324.

Legros (1978) Influence of vasopressin on memory and learning *Lancet* 7 Jan:41.

Joan Minninger (1984) *Total Recall* Ballantine p91.

Oliveros et al., (1978) Vasopressin and Amnesia *Lancet*, 7 Jan:42.

Melatonin, hydroxyl radical-mediated oxidative damage, and aging: A hypothesis (1993) *J. Pineal Res* 14:151-168

Melatonin in human cerebrospinal fluid: Its origin and variation with age. *Life Sci.*(1979) 25:929-936.

Plasma melatonin rhythm in normal aging and Alzheimer's Disease (1986) *J. Neural Transm.* Suppl.21:494

Alterations in nocturnal serum melatonin levels in humans with growth and aging (1988) *J. Clin. Endocrinol. Metab.* 66:648-652

Daily variation in the concentration of melatonin and 5-methoxy-tryptophol in the human pineal gland: Effect of age and Alzheimer's Disease (1990) *Brain Res.* 628:170-174

The pineal control of aging: The effects of melatonin and pineal grafting on the survival of older mice (1991) *Ann. N.Y. Acad. Sci.* 621:291-313

Pineal gland and aging (1991) *Aging* 3:103-116

The aging pineal gland and it's physiological consequences (1992) *Bioessays* 14:169-175

Concentrations of serotonin and its related substances in the cerebro-spinal fluid in patients with Alzheimer's type dementia (1992) *Neurosci. Lett.* 141:9-12

Pituitary-adrenocortical and pineal activities in the aged rat (1991) *Ann. N.Y. Acad. Sci.* 621:256-261

Antioxidant capacity of melatonin: A novel action not requiring a receptor (1993) *Neuroendocrinol. Lett.* 15:103-116

Melatonin and sleep in humans (1993) *J Pineal Res* 15:1-12

CHAPTER 17: MEDICATIONS AND MEMORY.

Greenblatt, D., et al. (1982) Drug Disposition in Old Age. *New England Journal of. Medicine* 306:1081-1088,

Williams, P., and Rush, D. (1986) Geriatric Polypharmacy. *Hospital Practice* Feb. 15.

Mangini, Richard J., ed. (1986) *Drug Interaction Facts* Lippincott, St. Louis.

Pearson, M. (1985) Prescribing for the elderly—An audit. *The Practitioner* 229:85-86, 1985.

Williamson, J., and Chopin, J. (1980) Adverse Reactions to prescribed Drugs in the Elderly: A multi-centre investigation." *Age and Ageing* 9:7380.

Farley, Dixie. Protecting the elderly from medication misuse. *FDA Consumer* 20(8):2831, 1986.

(1988) Globe-trotter's amnesia. (side effects of anti-jet-lag drug) v13 *Harvard Medical School Health Letter* Feb 13(2):6.

(1988) The case of jetsetter's amnesia. (Halcion induced amnesia) *Prevention* Jan 40(2):6.

(1988) Traveler's amnesia. (effect of triazolam on memory) v13 *Harvard Medical School Health Letter* March 13(1):8.

Kiyingi , K. (1993) How much do outpatients know about drugs prescribed to them? A pilot study. *PNG Med Journal* 36(1):29-32.

Kra, S. (1986) *Aging Myths: Reversible Causes of Mind and Memory Loss* McGraw-Hill, NY, p169.

Goodwin, F. (1991) Diazepam and memory loss. *JAMA, The Journal of the American Medical Association* August 28 266(1):1056

Cimetidine (Tagamet): (1978) Update on Adverse Effects. *Med Let.* 20:77- 78.

Schentag, J., et al. (1979) Pharmacokinetic and clinical studies in patients with cimetidine-associated mental confusion. *Lancet* 1:177 -181.

Basavaraju, N. (1980) Cimetidine-induced mental confusion in the elderly. *New York State J. Med.*, July 1287-1288.

Van Sweden, B., and Kamphusen, H. (1984) Cimetidine neurotoxicity. *Neurol.* 23:300-305.

Cerra, Frank B., et al. (1982) Mental Status, the intensive care unit, and cimetidine. *Annals of Surgery* 196:565-570.

Mani, R. (1984) H2-Receptor blockers and mental confusion. *Lancet* 2:98.

Fisher, C. (1992) Amnestic syndrome associated with propranolol toxicity: A case report. *Clinical Neuropharmacology,* 15 (5): 397 -403.

Leirer, V., Yesavage, J., Morrow, D. (1991) Marijuana carry-over effects on aircraft pilot performance. *Aviation Space and Environmental Medicine* 62(3):221-7.

Ghosh, S. (1976) Methyldopa and forgetfulness. *The Lancet* 1:202 -203

CHAPTER 18: NEUROTOXINS AND THE BRAIN

Commitee on Science & Technology (1989*) Neurotoxins at Home and the Workplace* U.S Government Printing Office, Washington, DC

Queen, H. (1988) *Chronic Mercury Toxicity* Queen & Co.

Warren, T.(1991) *Beating Alzheimer's* Avery Publishing Group Garden city Park, NY

Hodge, M. (1991) Getting the lead out. *Longevity*, May p14.(1989)

Marijuana mangles memory. v136 *Science News* Nov 18 136(1):332.

Farmanfarmanaian, R. (1990) Lead's new hideout:fast food brews. *Longevity* Jun. p15.

Domingo, J. et al. (1988) Citric, Malic and Succinic acid as possible alternatives to deferoxamine in aluminum toxicity. *Journal of Toxicology* 26(1-2):67-79

Chang, L. (1985) Neuropathological effects of toxic metal ions, in *Metal Ions in Neurology and Psychiatry* Liss, A., ed. p207.

Register, et al (1985) *Journal of the American Dietetic Assoc-iation* 61:159-162.

Douglas, J, et al (1985) The effects of a raw food diet on hypertension and obesity. *Southern Medical Journal* 78(7):841.

Horrobin, D. (1980) A biochemical basis for alcoholism and alcohol induced damage including the fetal alcohol syndrome and cirrhosis: Interference with essential fatty acids and prostaglandin metabolism. *Medical Hypothesis* 6:929:942.

Forander (1958) *Quarterly Journal of Studies on Alcohol* 19:379.

Kanazawa, S. & Herbert, V. (1985) total corinoid cobalamin (vitamin B_{12}) and cobalamin analogue levels may be normal in serum despite cobalamin in liver depletion in patients with alcoholism. *Lab Investigation* 53(1):108-110.

Bolla, K. (1993) Neurocognitive effects of aluminum. *Archives of Neurology* 49:1021-1026

Leo, M. & Lieber, C. (1983) Interaction of ethanol with vitamin A.

Garrett-Laster, M.(1984) Impairment of taste and olfaction in patients with cirrhosis: The role of vitamin A. *Human nutrition: Clinical nutrition* 38C:203-214.

Lieber, C. (1983) Alcohol Nutrition Interaction *Contemporary Nutrition.* Dec.

Loftis, Elizabeth (1980) *Alcohol, Marijuana, and Memory. Psychology Today,* March, pp42-56.

Lowe (1987) Combined effects of nicotine and Caffeine on State dependent learning. *Medical Science Research* 15: 25-26

Majumdar, S. (1981) Vitamin utilization status in chronic alcoholics. *International Journal of Vitamin and Nutrition Research* 51(1):54-58.

Thompson, A. & Majumdar, S. (1981) The influence of ethanol on intestinal absorption and utilization of nutrients.

Majundar, S..(1983) Vitamin A Utilization Status in Chronic Alcoholic Patients *International Journal of Vitamin and Nutrition Research* 53(3):273-279.

Sherlock, S. (1984) Nutrition and the Alcoholic *Lancet* 1:436-438.

CHAPTER 19: FREE RADICALS AND ANTIOXIDANTS

Reuben, C. (1995) *Antioxidants: Your Complete Guide* Prima Publishing

Free radicals in brain metabolism and pathology (1993) *British Medical Bulletin* 49:3;577-587

deJesus-Greenberg, D. (1981) Hyperbaric Oxygen Therapy *Critical Care Update* 8(2) 8-20.

Hyperbaric Oxygen Therapy: a Committee Report, Feb. 1981. Undersea medical Society, Inc. 9650 Rockville Pike, Bethesda Maryland 20014 (UMS Publication #30 CR(HBO)2-23-81).

Bjorksten, J. (1980) Possibilities and limitations of chelation as a means for life extension. *Rejuvenation* 8 67-72.

CHAPTER 20: DRUGS THAT IMPROVE MEMORY.

Bartus, R. et al (1981) Profound effects of combining choline and piracetam on memory enhancement and cholinergic function in aged rats *Neurobiology of Aging* 2:105-111.

Bartus R..& Dean, R. (1981) Age related memory loss and drug therapy: Possible directions based on animal models. *Aging* 17:209-223.

Bylinski, G. (1986) Medicine's next marvel: The memory pill *Fortune* Jan 20 p68-72.

Gutfeld, G.(1991) Memory pills-finally! Exciting new research promises the chance of regenerating failing memory banks. (phosphatidylserine may improve memory) *Prevention* August v43 p40(4)

Tipton, K. (1994) What is it that l-deprenyl (selegiline) might do? *Clin Pharmacol Ther* 56(6 Pt 2):781-96

Bartus R., et al. (1981) Profound effects of combining choline and piracetam on memory enhancement and cholinergic function in aged rats *Neurobiology of Aging* 2:105-111.

Friedman, E. (1981) Clinical response to choline plus piracetam in senile dementia: Relation to red cell choline levels *New England Journal of Medicine* 304 no 24, p1490-1491.

Ferris, S. (1982) Combination of Choline/Piracetam in the treatment of senile dementia *Psychopharmacology Bulletin* vol 18 p94-98.

Buresova, O. & Bures, J. (1976) piracetam-induced facilitation of interhemispheric transfer of visual information in rats *Psychopharmacologica* 46:93-102.

Chase, C. (1984) A new chemotherapeutic investigation: Piracetam effects on dyslexia *Annals of Dyslexia* 34:667-673.

Casey, D. & Denny, D. (1974) Dimethyl amino ethanol in tardive dyskinesia *New England Journal of Medicine* 291:797.

Casey, D. & Denny, D. (1979) Mood alterations During Deanol Therapy *Psychopharmacology* 62: 187-91.

Ceder, G. (1978) Effects of 2-Dimethylamonoethanol (Deanol) on the metabolism on choline in Plasma *Neurochemistry* 30::1293-1296.

Ansell, G. (1962) The Effects of 2-Dimehtylamono-ethanol on brain phospholipid metabolism *Journal of Neurochemistry* 9:253-263.

Copeland, R. (1981) Behavioral and neurochemical effects of Hydergine in rats *Archives of International Pharmacodynamics* 252:113-123.

Emmenegger, H., and Meier-Ruge, W. (1968) The Actions of Hydergine on the Brain *Pharmacology* 1 :65-78.

Exton-Smith, A. (1983) Clinical experience with ergot alkaloids *Aging* 23:323.

Diamond, S.& Bowers, E. (1976) Increase in the power of human memory in normal man through the use of drugs. *Psychopharmacology* 49:307-9.

Fanchamps, A. (1983) Dihidroergotoxin in senile Cerebral insufficiency *Aging* 23:311322

Dilanni, M. (1985) The Effects of Piracetam on Children with Dyslexia *Journal of Clinical Pharmacology* vol 5, p272-278.

Dimov, S. et. al. (1982) Neurophysiological Analysis of Piracetam Effect on Memory Processes. *Behavioral Brain Research* 5, no.1:98 -99.

Donaldson, T. (1984) Therapies to Improve Memory *Anti-Aging News* 4 no.: 13-21.

Giurgia, C. (1973) The Nootropic Approach to the Pharmacology of the Integrative Activity of the Brain *Conditioned Reflex* vol 8, no 2 p108-115.

Giurgia, C.(1980) A drug for the mind *Chemtech* jun p360-365.

Giurgia, C. & Salama, M. (1977) Nootropic drugs *Progress in Neuropsychopharmacology* (1):235-237.

Goldstien, et al, eds: (1980) *Ergot Compounds and Brain Function,* Raven Press.

Hindmarch, I. (1979) The effects of ergot alkaloid derivative (Hydergine) on aspects of psychomotor performance, arousal, and cognitive processing ability. *Journal of clinical Pharmacology* Nov :726-731.

Sandoz (no date) *Age related Mental Decline and Dementias: The Place for Hydergine* Products Literature Booklet.

Flood, J., et al.(1988) Dehydroepiandrosterone and its sulfate enhance memory retention in mice. *Brain Research* 447:269-278.

Rudman. D., et al. (1990) Plasma dehydroepiandrosterone sulfate in nursing home men.. *J. American Geriatr ic Soc* . 35: 421-427.

Bologa, L., et al. (1987) Dehydroepiandrosterone and its sulfated derivative reduce neuronal death and enhance astrocytic differentiation in brain call cultures. *J. Neuroscoience Research* 17:225-234.

Roberts, E., et al. (1987) Effects of dshydroepiandrosterone and its sulfate on brain tissue in culture and on memory in mice. *Brain Resear ch* 406:357-362.

Nasman, B., et al. (1991). Serum dehydroepiandrosterone sulfate in Alzheimer's disease and in multi-infarct dementia. *Biological Psychiatry* 30:684-690.

CHAPTER 21: VITAMINS THAT IMPROVE MEMORY

Barnes, M. (1975) The function of Ascorbic Acid in Collagen Metabolism *Annals of the New York Academy of Science* 258:264.

Bell, I. (1991) B_{12} folate balance improves mental state of elderly patients *Biological Psychiatry* 27:125-137.

Cone, W. (1983) *Effects of megadoses of Vitamin B_{12} on extinction in the rat*. Unpublished masters thesis California State University, Long Beach, CA.

(1979) Vitamin B_{12} Concentrations in Psychiatric patients *Acta Psychiatrica Scandinavia* 59: 145-152.

Lesser, M. (1980) *Nutrition and vitamin therapy* Bantam Books, New York.

Bieri, J. (1983) Medical Uses of Vitamin E *New England Journal of Medicine* 308:1063.

Holmes (1956) Cerebral Manifestations of Vitamin B_{12} Deficiency *British Medical Journal.*

Bober, M. (1984) Senile Dementia and Nutrition *British Medical Journal* 288:1234.

Cole, M. (1984) Low serum B_{12} in Alzheimer type dementia *Age & Ageing* 13:101-105.

Enk, C. (1980) Reversible dementia and neuropathy associated with folate deficiency 16 years after partial gastrectomy. *Scandanavian Journal of Haematology* 25:63.

Melamed, E. (1975) Reversable central nervous system dysfunction in folate deficiency. *Journal of Neurolgical Science* 25:93-98.

Strachan, R. & Henderson, J. (1967) Dementia and Folate Defiency *Quarterly Journal of Medicine* 36:189-204.

Sneath, P. (1973) Folate status in a geriatric population and its relation to dementia. *Age & Ageing* 2:177-182.

Shaw, D. (1984) Senile Dementia and Nutrition. *British Medical Journal* 288:792-793.

Keatinge, A. (1983) Vitamin B_1, B_2, B_6 and C status in the elderly. *Irish Medical Journal* 76:488-490.

CHAPTER 22: MINERALS THAT IMPROVE MEMORY

Pfeiffer, C. (1975) *Mental and Elemental Nutrients* Keats Publishing New Canaan, CT.

Erdmann, R. & Jones, M. (1988) *Minerals: Metabolic Miracle Workers* Century, London.

Passwater, R. (no date) *Selenium as Food and Medicine* Keats, NY.

(1970) Chromium Deficiency as a factor in Arteriosclerosis *Journal of Chronic Diseases* 23:12123-142.

Hambridge, E.(1974) Chromium Nutrition in Man *American Journal of Clinical Nutrition* 27(5):505-514.

Boyle, E. et al. (1977) Chromium Depletion in the Pathogenesis of Diabetes and Arteriosclerosis *Southern Medical Journal* 70(2):1449-1453.

Press, R., et al. (1990) The effect of chromium picolinate on serum cholesterol and apolipoprotein in human subjects. *Western Journal of Medicine* 152(1):41-45.

Mertz, W (1992) Chromium in human nutrition: A Review *Journal of Nutrition* 123:626-633.

Everson, G. & Schrader, R. (1968) Manganese *Journal of Nutrition* 94:89.

Clark, L (1985) The Epidemiology of Selenium in Cancer *Federal Proceedings* 44(9):2584-9.

Lerch, Sharon (1992) Memory boosters. (iron and zinc) *American Health* 11(2):129.

Emanuel, Linda (1991) Memory-boosting minerals. (iron and zinc) *Health* 23(1):22.

Hullin, R. (1983) Zinc levels in psychiatric patients. *Progress in Clinical and Biological Research* 129:197-206.

CHAPTER 23: NUTRIENTS THAT IMPROVE MEMORY

Brody (1975) RNA and memory *Aging* 1:153-155.

Odens (1970) RNA effects on memory

Harmon, D. (1993) Free radical Theory of Aging: A hypotheses on pathogenesis of senile dementia of the Alzheimer's type. *Age* 16:20-30.

Bland, J. (1982) Choline, Lecithin, Inositol and other 'Accessory' Nutrients. *Good Health Guide* 1:1-25.

Hoffer, A.& Walker, M. (1978) *Orthomolecular Nutrition*. Keats Publishing, New Canaan, Conn.

Sitaram, Weingartner, and Gillin (1978) Human serial learning: enhancement with arecoline and choline and impairment with scopolamine correlate with performance on placebo. *Science* 210: 274-76.

Sitaram, et al., (1978) Choline: Selective enhancement of low imagery words in man *Life Science*, 22:1555-1560.

(1990) *Arch Gerontol Geriatr*, 10:173-185

(1990) *Progress in Neuro Psychopharmacology & Biological Psychiatry* 1(4) :359-369

(1987) *Molecular Brain Research*, 3:55-60.

(1987) *Nature*, 329:6568

(1994) *Experimental Gerontology*, 29:55-66

Tucker, D.; Penland, J.; Sandstead, H. (1990) Nutrition Status and Brain Function in Aging *American Journal of Clinical Nutrition*

52:93-102.

CHAPTER 24: HERBS THAT IMPROVE MEMORY

Mowrey, D. (1986) *The Scientific Validation of herbal Medicine* Cormorant Books, Lehi, UT.

Lad, V. (1984) *Ayurveda: The Science of Self Healing - A Practical Guide*

Medicinal Plants of India (vol.1, 1976)

Bensky, D. & Gamble, A. (1986) *Chinese herbal Medicine: Materia Medica* Eastland Press, Seattle WA.

Duke, J. (1979) *CRC Handbook of Medicinal Herbs*

Halstead, B.& Hood. L. (1985) Eleutherococcus Senticosus- Siberian Ginseng: An Introduction to the concept of Adaptogenic Medicine *Clinical Trials Journal* 22.

Jackson, M. & Teague, T. (1987) *Handbook of Alternatives to Chemical Medicine* Bookpeople, Berkely, Ca.

Allard, M. (1986) Treatment of old age disorders with ginkgo biloba extract. *La Presse Medicale.* 15(31):1540.

Auguet, M., et al. (1986) Bases Pharmacologiques de 1'Impact Vasculaire de 1'Extract de Ginkgo Biloba," *La Presse Medicale.* 15(31):1524.

Funfgeld, E. (1989) A Natural and Broad Spectrum Nootropic Substance for Treatment of SDAT-- the Ginkgo Biloba Extract." *Progress in Clinical and Biological Research.* 317:1247-60

Gebner, A., et al. Study of the long-term action of a ginkgo biloba extract on vigilance and mental performance as determined by means of quantitative pharmaco-EEG and psychometric measurements. *Arzneimittelforschung.* 35(9):1459.

Hindmarch, I. (1986) Activity of ginkgo biloba extract on short-term memory. *La Presse Medicale.* 15(31): 1562- 1592.

Schaffer, K., Reeh, P. (1985) Long-term drug administration effects of ginkgo biloba on the performance of healthy subjects exposed to hypoxia. From Agnoli, J., *Effects of Ginkgo Biloba Extracts on Organic Cerebral Impairment.* Eurotext Ltd. pp77-84.

Warburton, D. (1986) Clinical psychopharmacology of ginkgo biloba Extract *La Presse Medicale.* 15(31):1595.

Harrer, G. & Sommel; H. (1994).Treatment of mild/moderate depressions with Hypericum. *Phytomedicine*; 1:3-8.

Hendler; S (1991). *The Doctors' Vitamin and Mineral Encyclopedia.* New York, NY: Simon and Schuster.

Hobbs, C. (1988). St. John's Wort: A Review. *HerbalGram* No. 18-19.

Hoffmann, J. & Kuhl, E. (1979).Therapie von depressiven Zustanden mit Hypericin (Treatment of depressive conditions with Hypericin). Z. *Allgemeinmed* 12:776-782.

Morauoni, P & Bombardellie, F: (1994). Hypericum perforatum. Milan, Italy. Indona.

SUGGESTED READING

Anderson, K., Anderson L. (1983) *Orphan Drugs* The Body Press, Los Angeles, CA.

Ayres, J. (1989) *Sensory Integration* Western Psychological Services, Los Angeles.

Baddeley, Allen (1982) *Your Memory: a users guide* Macmillan Publishing, NY.

Bailey, Herbert (1977) *GH3: Will it Keep You Young Longer?* Bantam Books, NY.

Batmanghelidj, F.(1995) *Your Body's Many Cries for Water* Global Health Solutions, Falls Church, VA.

Benson, D. (1985) *The Dual Brain* Guilford, NY.

Birren J. (1977) *Handbook of the Psychology of Aging* Van Nostrand Rhinehold, NY.

Birren, J.. & Cunningham, W. (1983) Psychology of Adult Development and Aging *Annual Review of Psychology* 34:543-575.

Bolles, Edmund (1988) *Remembering and Forgetting: Inquiries into he nature of memory* Walker and Company, NY.

Brynko, Barbara (1983) All About Memory *Science Digest* Nov. p71(7).

Casdorph, H. & Walker, M. (1995) *Toxic Metal Syndrome* Avery Publishing Group, Garden City Park, NY.

Cermak, L. (1972) *Human Memory: Research and Theory.* Ronald Press Co., NY.

Cheraskin, E. & Ringsdorf, W. (1974) *Psychodietetics* Stein and Day, NY.

Churchland, Patricia Smith, (1986) *Neurophilosophy* MIT Press, Bradford Books, Cambridge, Mass.

Coren, Stanley (1996) *Sleep Thieves* The Free Press, NY.

Daan, Serge & Gibber, Eberhard (no date) *Biological clocks and Environmental Time*

Dean, Ward & Morgenthaler, John (1990) *Smart Drugs & Nutrients* B&J Publications, Santa Cruz, CA.

de Weid, D. et. al. (1975) *Vasopressin and Memory Consolidation: Perspectives in Brain Research* Elsevier Scientific Publishing Company, New York.

Diamond, M (1988) *Enriching Heredity* The Free Press, NY.

Fidlow, Michael; (1984) *How to Strengthen Your Memory.* Gramercy Publishing, NY.

Figley and McCubbin (1983) *Stress and the Family* vol 2: Coping with Catastrophes N.Y., Bruner Mazel.

Flanigan, Owen J. (1984) *The Science of the Mind* MIT Press, Bradford Books, Cambridge, Mass.

Gazzaniga, Michael (1985) *The Social Brain* Basic Books, NY.

Gazzaniga, Michael (1988) *Mind Matters* Houghton Mifflin, Boston.

Goby, M..J. (1984) *Alcoholism: Treatment and Recovery* Catholic Health Association of the U.S., St. Louis. MO.

Gose, K. & Levi, G (1983) *Dealing with Memory Changes as You Grow Older* Bantam Books, NY.

Gordon, Barry (1995) *Memory* Mastermedia Limited, NY.

Graeden Joe (1980) *The People's Pharmacy-2* Avon, NY.

Herrmann, Douglas (1991) *Super Memory: A Quick Action Program for Memory Improvement* Rodale Press, Emmaus, PN.

Higbee, Kenneth L. (1977) *Your Memory: How it Works and How to Improve It.* Prentice Hall, NJ.

Ho et. al (1978) *Drug Discrimination and State Dependent*

Learning Academic Press, NY.

Hoffer, Abram, and Morton Walker (1978) *Orthomolecular Nutrition*. Keats Publishing, New Canaan, Conn.

Johnson, George (1991) *In the Palaces of Memory: How we build the world inside our heads* Alfred A. Knopf, NY.

Katzman, Robert; and R. Terry (1983) *The Neurology of Aging* F.A. Davis Company, Philadelphia.

Kra, S. (1986) *Aging Myths: Reversible Causes of Mind and Memory Loss* McGraw-Hill, NY.

Lesser, M. (1980) *Nutrition and Vitamin Therapy* Bantam Books, NY.

Loftis, Elizabeth (1980) *Memory* Addison-Wesley, Menlo Park, CA.

Lorayne, Harry, and Jerry Lucas (1982) *The Memory Book*. Ballentine Books, NY.

Lynch, Gary (1984) *Neurobiology of Learning and Memory* Guilford Press NY.

Martinez et al (1981) *Endogenous Peptides in the Learning and Memory Process* Academic Press, NY.

McDonough (1983) *Chelation Can Cure* Platinum Pen, KC, MO.

Mindell, Earl (1979) *Vitamin Bible* Rawson-Wade, NY.

Minninger, Joan (1984) *Total Recall* Pocket Books, NY.

Minskey, Marvin (1987) *The Society of Mind* Simon & Schuster, NY.

Morgan, Brian & R. Morgan,(1987) *Brainfood* The Body Press, Tucson, AZ.

Morgan, Brian (1987) *Nutrition Prescription* Crown Publishers.

Palombo, Stanley R.; (1978) *Dreaming and Memory*. Basic Books, NY.

Pearson, Durk, and Sandy Shaw (1982) *Life Extension* Warner Books, NY.

Pelton, Ross; (1986) *Mind Food and Smart Pills*. T&R Publishers, San Diego.

Pfeiffer, Carl C. (1975) *Mental and Elemental Nutrients* Keats Publishing, New Canaan, Conn.

Philpott, William & Kalita, Dwight (1980) *Brain Allergies: The Psychonutrient Connection* Keats Publishing, New Canaan, CT.

Rappoport, David (1961) *Emotions and Memory*. Science Editions Inc., NY.

Reuben, Carolyn (1995) *Antioxidants: Your Complete Guide* Prima Publishing, Rocklin, CA.

Saltin, B. Karlsson, J. (1971) *Muscle Metabolism During Exercise* Plenum Publishing, NY.

Schacter, Daniel, (1996) *Searching for Memory: the brain, the mind, and the past* Basic Books, NY.

Schuckit, Marc A. (1984) *Drug and Alcohol Abuse: A Clinical Guide To Diagnosis and Treatment* Plenum Press, NY.

Seamon, John G. (1980) *Memory and Cognition* Oxford University Press, NY.

Seiden and Dykstra, (1977) *Psychopharmacology: A Biochemical and Behavioral Approach.* Van Nostrand- Rhinehold.

Shnour, Elie (1974) *The Malnourished Mind* Anchor Press, Doubleday, NY.

Squire, Larry (1987) *Brain and Memory* Oxford University Press, NY.

Thompson, Richard F. (1985) *The Brain* W. H. Freeman & Co. San Francisco.

Walker, Morton (1982) *Chelation Therapy* Freelance Communications, Stamford Conn.

Watson, George (1972) *Nutrition and Your Mind* Harper and Row, NY.

Weinberger, Norman (1985) *Memory Systems of the Brain* Guilford NY.

Weinland, James (1957) *How to Improve Your Memory.* Barnes & Noble, NY.

Williams, Roger (1971) *Nutrition Against Disease* Pittman Publishing, NY.

Winter, A and Winter, R (1988) *Eat Right, Be Bright* St. Martin's Press, NY.

Wurtman R.J. (1982) *Nutrients that Modify Brain Function Scientific American* 246:50-59.

Zechmeister, Eugene B., and Stanley Nyberg (1982) *Human Memory* Brooks Cole, Monterey, CA.

INDEX

About the Author

As well as being a Licensed Psychologist, Dr. Cone is a consultant, an accomplished speaker, an author, and founder and director of the Sound Minds Institute in Beverly Hills, California. He specializes in memory problems. He is the author of two books, *Stop Memory Loss*, a book about aging and memory, and *Total Quality Care*, a book for professional caregivers of the aged.

Dr. Cone has written and produced training manuals, training tapes and record keeping systems for several direct-marketing companies and a national telecommunications company. He has developed memory improvement programs and wellness programs for many national corporations.

Dr. Cone's stress management seminars have been presented to police departments throughout the entire state of California. At the request of the California State Government he developed, designed, and implemented a training program for the California Conservation Corps that reduced the dropout rate by 26% in just six weeks!

Dr. Cone is currently a consultant in the field of geriatrics. He develops and implements training programs for geropsychiatric hospitals, nursing homes, and board & care facilities throughout the nation.

Because of his expertise he has been featured on many television programs including "Hard Copy," "Unsolved Mysteries," "The Maury Povitch Show," "Strange Universe," Toronto's "Fifth Estate," and is a frequent guest on the Learning Channel's new series, "Unnatural History." He has been a featured speaker on dozens of radio programs nationwide. His audio presentations are used all over the globe.

For more information about Dr. Cone's services and seminars, call (888) 261-0576.